COLOURS
OF SHETLAND

Puffin Sweater

Contents

Northmavine Hoody

Ursula Cardigan

Scatness Tunic

Stevenson Gauntlets

Colours of Shetland

Over the past few years, I have spent many happy months in Shetland. I am lucky enough, as a writer and designer, to have a job that often takes me north and these 'work' visits have also allowed me plenty of time to explore the varied landscape of this beautiful archipelago. I have loved walking in Shetland, learning about its history and culture, discovering its unique textile traditions at first-hand and writing about these traditions for many different publications. Though I would jump at the chance to live there, I currently spend most of my days in north Edinburgh: three hundred miles from Shetland, but still importantly connected to it.

During the Nineteenth Century, the population of Shetland was surprisingly mobile and dispersed. As with any island culture, the sea was a thoroughfare of connection, and one of the busiest Shetland thoroughfares was that which brought its community south to Edinburgh and Leith. Shetlanders followed the herring, worked for one of the many shipping companies or were employed by merchants whose dockside warehouses were, by the 1870s, stuffed full of the fine handiwork of the islands' knitters.

Over the latter part of the century, poor harvests and, in some areas of Shetland, clearances, meant that many islanders were forced permanently from 'da auld rock' to new homes in Leith and Bonnington, Broughton and Newhaven. By the turn of the Twentieth Century, these parts of the city had become a sort of 'little Shetland' – a fact that is immediately evident from a brief glance at city directories, with their long lists of familiar Shetland surnames. Shetlanders flocked together in Edinburgh as a strong community, supporting each other and forming clubs and associations that still thrive in these areas of the city.

Today, as I walk about North Edinburgh and Leith, I see these Shetland connections all over the streets in which I live. Elsewhere in the city there are other reminders, like The Meadows' great whalebone arch, commemorating the talented knitters who wowed visitors to the 1886 exhibition, or the Northern Lighthouse Board on George Street, which monitors Shetland's signature lights, built by the Stevenson family.

Though I am often absent from it, Shetland has a singular sort of presence for me and it serves as a constant source of inspiration for my work. Speaking personally, I find that, in one way or another, inspiration generally arises from memory or longing: as TS Elliot puts it in *East Coker*, 'Where you are is where you are not'. This book, then, was made in Edinburgh, but inspired by Shetland. Perhaps one day I will make a book in Shetland that has been inspired by Edinburgh.

Colours of Shetland is constructed around five sections or 'stories', each of which takes a different and distinctive palette as its theme. These sections allow you to explore my colour inspiration through words, photographs and a pair of designs. Each colour story showcases the rich and varied palette of Jamieson & Smith Jumper Weight. This flagship yarn – grown, sheared, sorted, graded and sold locally – has a genuine connection to the landscape in which it is produced and helps crofters to keep native sheep on the hill. I hope that knitting with Shetland yarns and exploring my Shetland colour stories allows you to experience a little of the magic of these inspiring islands.

It was important for me to combine writing and designing as I find they are both part of the same process: both involve the productive thrill of making something, while both balance discipline with creativity. In so many ways, this book feels like 'me', and that has made it a genuine pleasure to produce. I hope you enjoy it too.

Happy knitting,

Kate x

Jamieson & Smith's flagship Shetland yarn has a genuine connection to the landscape in which it is produced.

Northern Lights

Whether approaching the islands by sea or air, your first view of Shetland is likely to include a Stevenson lighthouse.

hetland is in many ways a liminal place, existing on the elemental boundary between land and sea. It has more coastline per square mile than anywhere else in Britain and there are few locations where salt water so powerfully defines the terms of everyday life. Standing on the borderline between sea and land are Shetland's lighthouses, iconic guardians of its rocky shores which, since the early decades of the Nineteenth Century, have protected countless seafarers from coming to grief in treacherous waters. Shetland currently has a total of thirty-four lights: twenty-four minor and ten major. Counted among the latter are the seven signature lights which began to be constructed almost two centuries ago by the pioneering engineers of the Stevenson family.

A FAMILY ENTERPRISE

The 'Lighthouse Stevensons' were several generations of Edinburgh engineers, beginning with Robert Stevenson (1772-1850). In 1787, Robert went into partnership with his stepfather Thomas Smith, who was developing a series of fixed lights to replace the fallible and poorly regulated beacons, which at the time lit up Scotland's coast. Robert revealed himself to be an accurate modeller, talented engineer and indefatigable businessman, leading to his appointment as chief executive of the Northern Lighthouse Board (NLB). In their employ, he

designed and constructed eighteen lighthouses in some of Scotland's wildest coastal locations, including, in 1821, the light at Shetland's Sumburgh Head.

Robert's sons, Alan, David and Thomas (father of *Treasure Island's* Robert Louis) all followed in their father's engineering footsteps, adding Out Skerries (1854), Muckle Flugga (1854-6) and Bressay (1858) to the family's Shetland total. In their turn, David's two sons, Charles and David A, continued the Stevenson's involvement with the flagship lighthouses of the north, erecting Fair Isle's North and South lights (1892), and finally Eshaness (1929), which was the last NLB lighthouse to be designed by a member of the Stevenson family.

THE 'GREAT PRECIPICE'

All of Shetland's lighthouses presented the Stevensons with particular challenges of construction, but perhaps none more so than Muckle Flugga. A sixty-foot tower atop a two-hundred-foot rock repeatedly battered by gale-force winds and waves, this lighthouse is Britain's most northerly and perhaps its most spectacularly located. Proposals to develop a lighthouse off Unst were first mounted during the Crimean War, when the British Admiralty were keen to find a northern route to expedite the Navy's safe passage to the Russian White Sea ports. David Stevenson was commissioned to investigate the options, tried to land twice on the 'great precipice', and failed, concluding that, 'it is not practicable to erect and maintain a lighthouse upon these rocks'.

The Admiralty, however, remained insistent and matters were decided in their favour when a group of officials were despatched from Trinity House (the Lighthouse authority of England and Wales), enjoying easy sailing out from Unst on an unusually calm and windless day. A temporary light was constructed and lit in October 1854, but the wild winter sea rose above the height of the rock and broke against the tower, putting the lives of the keepers at serious risk. In 1856, David and Thomas Stevenson began work on establishing a permanent lighthouse on Muckle Flugga, getting round the problem of the lack of locally accessible stone by shipping out bricks in small loads from Unst and throwing them ashore. The

new lighthouse was completed by the end of 1857 and, despite the many challenges thrown at it by a century and a half of Shetland weather, remains solid and watertight to this day.

DEFENCE AND ATTACK

Lighthouses are perhaps definitive symbols of the defence of humanity, but they can also be targets of human attack. During the Second World War, those in Shetland were repeatedly bombed, and none more severely than the two lights at Fair Isle. After a raid on the South Lighthouse in December 1941, Catherine Sutherland, the young wife of an assistant keeper, was killed and the following month saw raids of increasing severity.

On January 21st, 1942, a bomb directly hit the keepers' accommodation, which caught fire and burnt to the ground. Three people were killed, including William Morris, who had been manning an anti-aircraft gun nearby. When news of the South Lighthouse disaster reached the North Lighthouse, assistant keeper Roderick Macaulay battled his way through gale-force winds and driving snow for three miles to restore the light to working order, before returning again on foot to cover his own watch. The keepers' accommodation at the South Light was reconstructed, but evidence of the raids can still be seen in craters beyond the lighthouse walls.

Fair Isle's South Lighthouse was the last in Britain to be automated. On 31st March, 1998, the final keeper left the building, and, like other Scottish lights, that at South Fair Isle began to be monitored remotely from Edinburgh by the NLB. Today, several of Shetland's Stevenson lighthouses have been renovated, offering pleasant holiday accommodation in spectacular locations. At Sumburgh Head, the lighthouse is now part of an impressive Shetland Amenity Trust project, due to open to the public in its fully restored state in 2014.

SHETLAND'S SENTINELS

For almost two centuries, Shetland's Stevenson lighthouses have captured the imaginations of innumerable artists, writers and photographers. Perhaps because of their wild locations, perhaps because their very shape and structure conveys the idea of a lonely figure standing tall and defiant against the sea – there is something about them that speaks very powerfully to us. Their symbolism is Janus-faced: simultaneously calling up ideas of isolation and warm welcome; suggestive of an exposure that is bleak, inhuman, elemental, but also bringing to mind the distinctly human cheer of reaching land. Shining out against the darkness; enduring against seas, storms and enemy bombs, these buildings are the very image of steadfastness and perseverance.

Bright sentinels of Shetland, they have acted as figures of greeting for almost two centuries, and still do so today. If you are approaching from the air, your first glimpse of Mainland Shetland is likely to include the Sumburgh Lighthouse. If you are crossing by sea, it is the Bressay Light that beckons you ashore. To travellers, these structures simply signal a long-awaited arrival at one's final destination, but to a Shetlander returning to the islands from around the world, the first sight of a Stevenson light means 'home'.

DESIGNING STEVENSON

The starting point for my Stevenson designs was the colour yellow. If you are looking at any lighthouse around the coastline of Scotland or Shetland, you can generally tell whether or not it was designed by a Stevenson by its distinctive yellow paintwork.

This colour association was strongly reinforced on a visit to Sumburgh Head in January 2011, when I was struck by the bold patterns of a particular yellow lichen – *Xanthoria*

parietina – upon the walls of the lighthouse. The white render was decorated with crazy egg-yolk yellow squiggles: it was almost as if the lichen had 'caught' the shade of the paintwork at the top of the building and had decided to scrawl out grafitti with it around the lower walls.

A particular shade or hue can frequently suggest to me how built structures and the natural world co-exist and come to mutually define each other, and the relationship between the painted surfaces and colonising lichen of this iconic lighthouse seemed to sum that up. I began work with the gauntlets – which are tall and tubular, just like a lighthouse – and settled on a simple maritime design.

On both gauntlets and sweater, blue matelot stripes are alternated with flashes of gold in a single round of colourwork that is easily accomplished by any beginner to this technique. As well as the striking yellow lichen, and the distinctive yellow paintwork, these broken flashes are also meant to suggest the beam of the lamp of a Stevenson lighthouse as it turns.

RESOURCES

Bella Bathurst, *The Lighthouse Stevensons* (reissued edn, 2005)
Sharma Krauskopf, *Scottish Lighthouses* (2001)
Northern Lighthouse Board
www.nlb.org.uk
Shetland Lighthouse Holidays
www.shetlandlighthouse.com
Sumburgh restoration
www.sumburghhead.com

PHOTOGRAPHY

6   The Bressay Lighthouse
7   Fanciful depiction of Muckle Flugga from Robert Cowie's *Shetland: Descriptive and Historical* (1874)
8   TOP: The Out Skerries Lighthouse
     BOTTOM: Runic shapes in lichen
9   The Stevenson Sweater and Gauntlets
All images © Kate Davies Designs and www.shetland.org

Shining out against the darkness; enduring against seas, storms and enemy bombs, these buildings are the very image of steadfastness and perseverance.

STEVENSON SWEATER AND GAUNTLETS

With simple lines and a maritime theme, the colours of the Stevenson designs echo the paintwork and lichen that adorn these iconic lighthouses.

PATTERNS » SWEATER PAGE **12**, GAUNTLETS PAGE **16**

STEVENSON SWEATER

A neat, nautical tee, inspired by Shetland's maritime heritage.

SIZES

Stevenson is designed for a close fit, and should be worn with around 5cm/2in negative ease. I recommend picking the size just below your actual bust measurement.

TO FIT BUST

81	**86**	91	**97**	102	**107**	112	**117**	122	**127**	cm
32	**34**	36	**38**	40	**42**	44	**46**	48	**50**	in

ACTUAL BUST

76	**81**	86	**91**	96	**101**	106	**111**	117	**121**	cm
30	**31.75**	34	**35.75**	38	**39.75**	42	**43.75**	46	**47.75**	in

LENGTH TO UNDERARM

42	**42**	42	**44**	44	**45**	45	**46**	46	**46**	cm
16.5	**16.5**	16.5	**17.25**	17.25	**18**	18	**18**	18	**18**	in

ARMHOLE DEPTH (INCLUDING NECK EDGING)

21	**22**	24	**25**	26	**27**	27	**28**	28	**28**	cm
8.25	**8.75**	9.5	**9.75**	10.25	**10.5**	10.5	**10.75**	10.75	**10.75**	in

FINISHED LENGTH

63	**64**	66	**69**	70	**72**	72	**73**	73	**73**	cm
24.5	**25.25**	25.75	**27**	27.5	**28.5**	28.5	**28.75**	28.75	**28.75**	in

HIP

81	**86**	91	**96**	102	**106**	112	**117**	122	**127**	cm
32	**34**	36	**38**	40	**42**	44	**46**	48	**50**	in

WAIST

61	**66**	71	**76**	81	**86**	91	**96**	102	**106**	cm
24	**26**	28	**30**	32	**34**	36	**38**	40	**42**	in

MATERIALS

Jamieson & Smith 2 Ply Jumper Weight (100% Shetland Wool; 118m/25g balls)

MC: **SHADE 202**
5 (**6**, 6, **7**, 7, **8**, 8, **9**, 9, **9**) x 25g balls
CC1: **SHADE FC47**
1 (**1**, 2, **2**, 2, **2**, 2, **2**, 2, **2**) x 25g balls
CC2: **SHADE 91**
3 (**3**, 3, **3**, 4, **4**, 4, **4**, 4, **4**) x 25g balls

2.75mm (UK 12/US 2) circular needle in the following lengths:
1 x 60cm/24in long (for working body); 1 x 80-100cm/ 30-40in long (for working yoke)
2.5mm (UK 13-12/US 1-2) circular needle in the following lengths: 1 x 60cm/24in long (for working rib); 1 x 40cm/16in long (for working neck edging); 1 x 20cm/8in long or dpns (for working sleeve caps)
Spare needles or waste yarn for holding stitches
Stitch markers
Tapestry needle for weaving in ends

TENSION

Work a tension swatch as follows (or make a pair of Stevenson Gauntlets):
With MC, cast on **66** sts, pm, and join for working in the round.
Round 1: Reading from right to left, work from row 1 of chart, repeating motif 11 times in total (for row 1 simply knit with MC).
Continue to work in pattern as set by last round until piece measures 15cm/6in.
Cast off all sts.
Block your swatch and count the sts and rounds to 10cm/4in.

30 sts and 36 rounds to 10cm/4in over colourwork pattern using 2.75mm needles

You must match the correct tension, or your tee will not fit. If you have too many sts to 10cm/4in, then you need to use a larger needle. If you have too few sts to 10cm/4in, then you need to use a smaller needle. In either case you will need to prepare a new tension swatch as described above.

ABBREVIATIONS

See full list of abbreviations on page 87.

KEEPING PATTERN CORRECT

This sweater features a simple 6 round design, involving one striped round (round 4) and a single round of stranded colourwork (round 6). In the written instructions, you will occasionally be told to 'keep pattern correct'. What this means is that:

1 The pattern should always be worked over a 6 round sequence (so if you finish knitting the body on a round 4, you will begin knitting the yoke on a round 5).
2 Shaping (increases and decreases) should always be worked on odd rounds (rounds 1, 3 or 5).
3 When you work a round 6 after shaping has taken place, ensure that your blocks of 3 yellow stitches **always** line up with those in the rounds below.
4 Treat each section of shaping separately (ie, when working waist shaping the pattern over the front sts is treated separately from the back sts, and when working the raglan shaping, the sleeves, front and back sts are all treated separately). With a simple pattern like this, it doesn't matter if a section ends with a partial repeat.
If you always follow rule 3, rule 4 will follow.

INSTRUCTIONS

1

CAST ON, ESTABLISH RIB, PLACE SIDE MARKERS

With CC2 and 2.5mm circular needle (60cm/24in long), cast on 240 (**254**, 270, **284**, 300, **314**, 330, **344**, 360, **374**) sts, pm, and join for working in the round.
Round 1: *K1, p1* repeat from * to * to end.
Last round sets 1x1 rib.
Round 2: Work 120 (**127**, 135, **142**, 150, **157**, 165, **172**, 180, **187**) sts in rib, pm, rib to end of round (markers now set position of side shaping).
Cont to work in 1x1 rib for 10 (**10**, 10, **13**, 13, **13**, 13, **18**, 18, **18**) more rounds.

2

BEGIN WAIST DECREASES

Keeping rib pattern correct, work decreases as follows:
A: *Work 1 st, k2tog, rib to 3 sts before marker, ssk, work 1 st, slm* repeat from * to * once more.
B: Work 3 rounds in rib.
Repeat steps A and B 4 more times. 220 (**234**, 250, **264**, 280, **294**, 310, **324**, 340, **354**) sts

3

BEGIN MAIN PATTERN, CONTINUE WAIST DECREASES

Change to 2.75mm circular needle (60cm/24in long) and MC, begin working from chart row 1 (repeating motif across round) and, keeping pattern correct, continue working waist decreases as follows:
A: *K1, k2tog, k to 3 sts before marker, ssk, k1, slm* repeat from * to * once more.
B: K 3 rounds.
Repeat steps A and B 9 more times. 180 (**194**, 210, **224**, 240, **254**, 270, **284**, 300, **314**) sts.
Work in pattern for a further 2.5cm/1in, ending with a chart round 2, 4 or 6.

4

WORK BUST INCREASES

Keeping pattern correct and always working shaping on odd-numbered chart rounds, work bust increases as follows:
A: *K1, m1, k to 1 st before marker, m1, k1, slm* repeat from * to * once more.
B: K 5 rounds.
Repeat steps A and B 10 more times. 224 (**238**, 254, **268**, 284, **298**, 314, **328**, 344, **358**) sts.

Work 1 (**1**, 1, **5**, 5, **11**, 11, **7**, 7, **7**) more rounds without further shaping, thus ending on a chart round 1, 3 or 5. Piece should measure 42 (**42**, 42, **44**, 44, **45**, 45, **46**, 46, 46) cm/16.5 (**16.5**, 16.5, **17.25**, 17.25, **18**, 18, **18**, 18, 18) in from cast-on edge.

5 SET UNDERARM STS ASIDE

Moving sts around needle without knitting, slip 7 (**7**, 7, **7**, 8, **8**, 8, **9**, 9, **10**) sts each side of each marker to waste yarn. Two sets of 14 (**14**, 14, **14**, 16, **16**, 16, **18**, 18, **20**) sts set aside for underarms and two sets of 98 (**105**, 113, **120**, 126, **133**, 141, **146**, 154, **159**) sts for front/back remain.
Set aside body sts.

6 WORK SLEEVE CAPS, SET UNDERARM STS ASIDE

With CC2 and 2.5mm circular needle (20cm/8in long or dpns), cast on 80 (**84**, 88, **92**, 96, **100**, 104, **108**, 112, **116**) sts, pm, and join for working in the round.
Work in 1x1 rib, as set on body for 15 rounds.

Now, moving sts around needles without knitting, slip 7 (**7**, 7, **7**, 8, **8**, 8, **9**, 9, **10**) sts each side of marker to waste yarn. 14 (**14**, 14, **14**, 16, **16**, 16, **18**, 18, **20**) sts set aside at underarm and 66 (**70**, 74, **78**, 80, **84**, 88, **90**, 94, **96**) sleeve-cap sts remain.
Set aside. Make another sleeve cap in the same way.

7 JOIN BODY AND SLEEVE CAPS INTO YOKE, WORK RAGLAN DECREASES

With 2.75mm circular needle (80-100cm/30-40in long), and **keeping pattern correct**, join body and sleeve caps into yoke as follows:
Next round: K98 (**105**, 113, **120**, 126, **133**, 141, 146, 154, **159**) sts of back, pm, k66 (**70**, 74, **78**, 80, **84**, 88, **90**, 94, **96**) of left sleeve, pm, k98 (**105**, 113, **120**, 126, **133**, 141, **146**, 154, **159**) sts of front, pm, k66 (**70**, 74, **78**, 80, **84**, 88, **90**, 94, **96**) of right sleeve, pm for start of round. 328 (**350**, 374, **396**, 412, **434**, 458, **472**, 496, **510**) sts. Begin working raglan decreases as follows:
A: *K1, k2tog, k to 3 sts before marker, ssk, k1, slm* repeat from * to * 3 more times.
8 sts decreased.
B: K 1 round.
Repeat steps A and B 21 (**24**, 27, **29**, 31, **30**, 28, **30**, 27, **25**) more times. 152 (**150**, 150, **156**, 156, **186**, 226, **224**, 272, **302**) sts.

Sixth to tenth sizes only
C: *K1, k3tog, k to 4 sts before marker, sssk, k1, slm* repeat from * to * 3 more times.
16 sts decreased.
D: K 1 round.
Repeat steps C & D - (-, -, -, -, **1**, 3, **3**, 6, **8**) more times. - (-, -, -, -, **154**, 162, **160**, 160, **158**) sts.

First, fourth, fifth, eighth and ninth sizes only
Next round: *K1, k2tog, k to marker, slm, k to marker, slm* repeat from * to * once more. 150 (-, -, **154**, 154, -, -, **158**, 158, -) sts.

Seventh size only
Next round: *K1, k2tog, k to marker, slm* repeat from * to * 3 more times. 158 sts.

Second, third, sixth and tenth sizes only
Next round: K to end.

All sizes
Remove all markers, except start of round marker. You should now have 150 (**150**, 150, **154**, 154, **154**, 158, **158**, 158, **158**) sts.

8 WORK SHORT ROWS

Before beginning next step, familiarise yourself with the instructions for short rows in the **Special Techniques** section on page 84.

Change to 2.5mm circular needle (40cm/16in long) and CC2.
Sizes are listed in the table from left to right (see below). Select the relevant column for your size, then work as follows.

Short row 1 (RS): Beginning at start of round, work in 1x1 rib as set on body over the number of sts in first row for your size, then turn.
Short row 2 (WS): Work in 1x1 rib as set over the number of sts in the second row for your size, turn.
Last 2 rows set 1x1 rib short rows. Cont to work short rows from table as set, until all rows for your size are complete.

Next round (partial): Work in 1x1 rib to end of round marker, closing gaps of all short rows.
Next round: Work in 1x1 rib for a complete round, closing gaps of all short rows.

9 WORK NECK EDGING

Work in 1x1 rib for 16 rounds.
Bind off all sts using your favourite stretchy bind-off method (see **Special Techniques**, page 84).

10 FINISHING

Graft sts at underarms together using Kitchener Stitch (see **Special Techniques**). Weave in all ends to the back of the work. Soak garment in tepid water with wool wash to allow the sts to relax and bloom. Rinse carefully in cold water. Press garment between towels to remove water Shape garment to correct dimensions and pin out flat, or dry over dress form. Leave to dry completely.

Enjoy your Stevenson Sweater!

KEY

□ MC (202); Knit
■ CC1 (FC47); Knit
□ CC2 (91); Knit

CHART

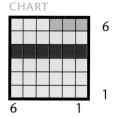

SHORT ROW SHAPING

	FIRST	SECOND	THIRD	FOURTH	FIFTH	SIXTH	SEVENTH	EIGHTH	NINTH	TENTH
Row 1	60	61	63	66	68	69	73	74	76	77
Row 2	66	67	69	72	74	75	79	80	82	83
Row 3	64	65	67	70	72	73	77	78	80	81
Row 4	62	63	65	68	70	71	75	75	78	79
Row 5	60	61	63	66	68	69	73	74	76	77
Row 6	58	59	61	64	66	67	71	72	74	75
Row 7	56	57	59	62	64	65	69	70	72	76
Row 8	54	55	57	60	62	63	67	68	70	71
Row 9	none	none	none	none	60	61	65	66	68	69
Row 10	none	none	none	none	58	59	63	64	66	67
Row 11	none	none	none	none	none	none	none	none	64	65
Row 12	none	none	none	none	none	none	none	none	62	63

STEVENSON GAUNTLETS

Simple-to-knit stripy gauntlets to keep your hands and wrists cosy in chill sea breezes. Use these as a swatch for working the Stevenson sweater.

SIZE
One size only
Hand circumference above thumb: 20cm/8in
Length: 28cm/11.5in
The hand circumference can easily be adjusted, if required, by adding or removing multiples of the 6-st pattern repeat. Don't forget that you will need to adjust your yarn quantities to reflect any changes.

MATERIALS
Jamieson & Smith 2 Ply Jumper Weight (100% Shetland Wool; 118m/25g balls)
    MC: SHADE 202
        2 x 25g balls
    CC1: SHADE FC47
        1 x 25g ball
    CC2: SHADE 91
        1 x 25g ball
3mm (UK 11/US2-3) circular needle in the following length:
1 x 20cm/8in long or dpns
2.75mm (UK 12/US 2) circular needle in the following length:
1 x 20cm/8in long
2.75mm (UK 12/US 2) dpns (for thumb)
Stitch markers
Waste yarn (a smooth cotton 4 ply will work best as it won't stick to your main yarn)
Tapestry needle for weaving in ends

TENSION
30 sts and 36 rounds to 10cm/4in over colourwork pattern using 2.75mm needles
28 sts and 34 rounds to 10cm/4in over colourwork pattern using 3mm needles

ABBREVIATIONS
See full list of abbreviations on page 87.

INSTRUCTIONS

1

CAST ON, ESTABLISH RIB

With CC2, and 2.75mm needles cast on 60 sts, pm, and join for working in the round.
Round 1: *K1, p1* repeat from * to * to end.
Last round sets 1x1 rib. Work in 1x1 rib for 15 more rounds.

Change to 3mm needles.
Round 17: Reading from right to left, work from row 1 of chart, repeating motif 10 times in total. Last round sets chart pattern. Work until chart row 6 is complete. Then work chart rows 1-6 three more times.

Change to 2.75mm needles and work chart rows 1-6 eight more times.

2

THUMB PLACEMENT

Change to 3mm needles.
Next round: K8 using waste yarn, slip these 8 sts back onto left needle, and knit to end of round with MC (chart row 1).
You will now have 8 sts of waste yarn in your fabric. After completion of the hand, you will come back to these stitches, unpick the waste yarn, and work an 'afterthought' thumb.

3

WORK HAND, BIND OFF

Work chart rows 2-6, then work 2 more repeats, thus ending with chart row 6.
Knit 1 round in MC.

Change to 2.75mm needles and CC2.
Work in 1x1 rib as set at start for 9 rounds.
Bind off all sts.

4

THUMB

With CC2 and 2.75mm dpn, pick up (but don't knit) 8 sts in row of sts below waste yarn. With second 2.75mm dpn, pick up (but don't knit) 8 sts in row of sts above waste yarn. Carefully remove waste yarn. Now join in yarn at start of lower needle, k8 from first dpn, pick up and knit 2 sts in gap between needles, k8 from second dpn, pick up

and knit 2 sts in gap, pm for start of round. 20 sts. Redistribute sts on needles as desired. Work in 1x1 rib as set at start for 6 rounds.
Bind off all sts.

5

SECOND GAUNTLET

Work step 1 as for first gauntlet.

6

THUMB PLACEMENT

Change to 3mm needles.
Next round: With MC, k to last 8 sts, k8 using waste yarn, slip these 8 sts back onto lh needle, and knit to end of round with MC (chart row 1). You will now have 8 sts of waste yarn in your fabric. After completion of the hand, you will come back to these stitches, unpick the waste yarn and work an 'afterthought' thumb.

7

COMPLETE SECOND GAUNTLET

Complete second gauntlet by working steps 3 and 4, as for first gauntlet.

8

FINISHING

With tapestry needle, weave in all ends, paying particular attention to the thumb join which may need neatening. Soak gauntlets in tepid water and wool wash, then press between towels. Shape gauntlets to finished dimensions. Lie flat and allow to dry fully.

Enjoy your Stevenson Gauntlets!

KEY

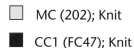 MC (202); Knit

CC1 (FC47); Knit

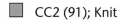 CC2 (91); Knit

CHART

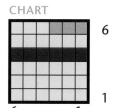

On the naming of Puffins

Colourful and appealing, Shetland's iconic bird is known by an intriguing variety of names around the coasts of Ireland and Great Britain.

The *Puffin* – or the *Tammie Norrie* – is a bird immediately associated with Shetland. In the early summer months, thousands of puffins leave the chilly waters of the Arctic Circle, put on their summer colours, and return to Shetland for the breeding season. And, in their turn, hundreds of human visitors flock to Shetland just to see the puffins: the opportunity to observe these lovely birds from relatively close quarters at Sumburgh and Hermaness being just too good to miss.

For who doesn't love a puffin? Sociable, curious, characterful and colourful: even those with the merest passing interest in Shetland's wildlife seem to find these birds immensely appealing.

It is perhaps because of its spectacularly shaded beak – the outer parts of which are shed each winter leaving a smaller, duller bill behind – that the puffin is immediately recognisable. Indeed, it is probably due to its remarkable appearance that, over the centuries, the humble puffin has come to be known by a dizzying number and variety of local names around the coasts of Ireland and Great Britain. So, what do the names *Puffin* and *Tammie Norrie* really mean?

SOFT, FAT FELLOWS

The origin of the name *Puffin* is a matter of some debate. John Caius (1570) argued that 'pupin' referred to the sound made by the bird, but the *Oxford English Dictionary* and a number of reliable ornithological sources seem to agree that, in one way or another, the name 'puffin' comes from 'puff' – meaning swollen or fleshy and, in this context, good for eating. In some early European texts, *Puffins* are interchangeable with *Manx Shearwaters* (for whom the French name is *Puffin des Anglais*) and indeed both species were frequently salted or pickled by coastal communities, and traded as food.

Most discussions of puffins before 1800 refer to the fact that around the coasts of Great Britain many folk regarded puffins as 'half fish, half flesh' and 'esteemed them a delicacy'. One Gaelic name for a young puffin – *Gille Bog*, meaning 'soft fat fellow' – certainly suggests a tasty, edible creature. In fact, puffins are still preserved and eaten in some Northern Atlantic communities, such as Iceland and the Faroe Islands.

For the puffin's standard scientific name, *Fratercula arctica*, we must thank Conrad Gessner, who, in his *Historia Animalium* (1551-1558) wrote:

> *'If you imagine that this bird was white, and had then put on a black cloak with a cowl, you would give this bird the name of* Fratercula Marina, *[the little friar of the sea].'*

This description apparently enraged John Caius, who, considering the 'little friar' to be whimsical and silly, struck the name out of his own copy of Gessner's book. But the puffin's

Tammie Norrie

Seamus Ruadh

Reid Nebbit

Buthaid

Tammie Cheekie

Fachach

Cockandy

Gille Bog

Bass Cock

Albanach

Ailsa Cock

Coulterneb

Éan Dearg

Pibbin

Patie

Canog

Pwffin

Puifin

Pâl

Mullet

Fuipín

Helegug

Bottlenose

Tommy Noddy

Guldenhead

Lundy Parrot

Willock

Nath

Pope

Popey Duck

is known as *Lundy Parrot*. This name combines the *Lund* root, which means *Puffin* in a number of different Scandinavian languages, with *Sea Parrot*, the name by which the bird is known in most Mediterranean countries.

DIMINUTIVE AND FOOLISH

And what, then, of *Tammie Norrie,* the name by which the puffin is affectionately known in Shetland and Orkney? Many Shetland dialect names for birds are Norn, but *Tammie Norrie*'s origin is Scots. The name's first reliable cited appearance in reference to the puffin is 1701, and subsequently *Tammie Norrie* is a name with commonplace and widespread usage throughout Shetland, as well as the whole of East and Lowland Scotland, throughout the Eighteenth and the Nineteenth centuries.

'Tam' [Tom], is a generic Scots name for a bloke or man and poor old *Tammie Norrie* seems to have been a singularly stupid one. Associated in various regional folk tales and poems with a particularly dimwitted Fife cowherd who was turned to stone by an irritable ghost, or a bashful Lothian suitor who failed to get the girls, *Tammie Norrie* was a name that could be applied to any chap who seemed particularly daft, clumsy or diminutive in either attitude or stature. To be compared to a *Tammie Norrie* was not in any way a compliment but was rather a suggestion that one was vacuous or inane.

Anglicised into *Tommy Noddy, Tomnoddy,* or *Tom Noddle,* the name made its way into Victorian English in association with the puffin as stupid fellow or fool. While these connotations of stupidity may have faded, and the name *Tammie Norrie* is now only ever used in reference to a puffin with affection rather than disdain, it is nonetheless surprising how many reliable sources still associate the bird with ideas of stupidity or lack of dignity, or use words such as 'grotesque' in reference to its appearance (Lockwood, 1984).

association with men of the cloth endured, not just in works of taxonomy, but through everyday usage in oral and folk cultures around the coasts of Ireland and Great Britain. In Cornwall, puffins are still known as *Pope* or *Popey-Duck* while in some parts of Ireland the bird is referred to as an *Albanach* – a word not simply meaning *Scotsman*, but also *Presbyterian*. When one considers the many ways in which religion can define and divide communities, one wonders how many other local names for wildlife might have been used colloquially to express identity or difference?

SPADE-NOSED BIRDS

Many local names for the puffin draw on the shape of its distinctive beak. The bird was once widely-known as *Coulterneb* in much of Northumbria and South-East Scotland – *Coulter* being the cutting blade of a traditional horse-drawn plough and *neb* meaning nose. In some parts of Wales, meanwhile, the puffin is referred to as *Pâl* or *Aderyn y Pâl* – the spade-nosed bird. In other northern communities, local nomenclature draws on the singular summer colours of the puffin: some Gaelic speakers know it as *Seamus Ruadh* [red Seamus], a name with a Scots equivalent in *Reid Nebbit* [red nose]. Further south, the puffin's regional names reveal a mingling of several different cultural influences: at Lundy Island in North Devon, for example, the bird

...the bright colours of their beaks are those of an optimistic 1920s palette.

MODERNIST ICONS

Tammie Norries are, in fact, not in the least inept, grotesque or daft. They are attractive, intriguing and well-adapted creatures: talented divers and swimmers; fiercely protective; determined fighters; loyal and sociable mates. Their appearance is incredibly striking. The structure of their marvellous beaks is suggestive of great icons of design: to me, they seem the Chrysler Buildings of the bird world. Decorated with hues and shapes that Sonia Delaunay and Wassily Kandinsky would surely have admired, the bright colours of their beaks are those of an optimistic 1920s palette.

Anyone who has watched a puffin at close quarters will have noticed their distinctive, stylised ways of moving for locomotion and display. Puffin colonies are alive with crazy moves and jazz rhythms as the birds crouch and shuffle, jerk and stomp. In terms of form, colour and rhythm, then, the puffin is to me the quintessential Modernist bird. My two designs are meant to showcase the bold and graphic beauty of the puffin in these terms.

As I researched the etymology of the puffin, the growing list of names began to take on a numinous quality, like the stations of the UK shipping forecast. With this in mind, I asked talented graphic designer Siân Brooks to produce a 'Puffin Forecast' map, illustrating the bird's regional nomenclature. I love the end result, which is suggestive of Ireland's and the UK's linguistic variation, as well as the way that local identities can be defined through the naming of things. I am also thrilled to be able to include the work of talented Shetland photographer, John Moncrieff, alongside my designs. What I particularly enjoy about John's images is that none of the creatures he photographs look *generic* – they are all, somehow, quite obviously individuals.

When I began work on the beak-inspired yoke of my puffin sweater, I used the deeply saturated, solid tones and hues that John had captured in his photographs to help me select yarn colours and place them in a chevron sequence. His pictures also made me think about the importance of texture to the shaded definition of puffins' beaks, something which I have tried to capture with the use of garter stitch and double decreases. I swatched the stitch pattern and shade sequence several times before I was completely happy with its 'puffin-ness', and the sweater that resulted is one of my favourite designs in this collection. Continuing the birdy-theme, 'mantle', is a word associated with avian anatomy, as well as being a traditional name for a short cloak or cape.

These two designs were produced in happy celebration of one of my favourite Shetland creatures. I do hope you like them.

AUTHOR'S NOTE

I discovered many more puffin names than those included on the map. My general rule when deciding on inclusion was that the name should be confirmed in two or more sources (eg, Ray's *Ornithologia* (1678); Dwelly's *Faclair Gàidhlig gu*

Beurla le Dealbhan, (1911) or Lockwood's *British Bird Names* (1984) cross-referenced with the most recent edition of the *Oxford English Dictionary*). In many cases, nomenclature was confirmed by dialect speakers from relevant regions.

RESOURCES

Tim Birkhead, *The Wisdom of Birds: An Illustrated History of Ornithology* (2008)
Mike P Harris and Sarah Wanless, *The Puffin* (2011)
W B Lockwood, *The Oxford Book of British Bird Names* (1984)

PHOTOGRAPHY

18   Puffin Portrait
19   The Puffin Forecast
20   TOP: Perched Puffin
       BOTTOM: Puffin Greetings
21   Puffin Mantle
All images © Kate Davies Designs and John Moncrieff

PUFFIN SWEATER AND PUFFIN MANTLE

A striped chevron pattern echoes the colours, shape and texture of the remarkable beaks that puffins display throughout the summer while visiting Shetland.

PATTERNS » SWEATER PAGE 24

MANTLE PAGE 30

PUFFIN SWEATER

A close-fitting sweater with a striking puffin-beak pattern across the yoke.

SIZES

The Puffin Sweater is designed for a close fit and should be worn with slight negative ease. I recommend picking the size just below your actual bust measurement for the best fit.

TO FIT BUST

81	**86**	91	**97**	102	**107**	112	**117**	122	**127**	cm
32	**34**	36	**38**	40	**42**	44	**46**	48	**50**	in

ACTUAL BUST

80	**85**	89	**95**	99	**105**	110	**115**	122	**129**	cm
31.5	**33.5**	35	**37.5**	39	**41.5**	43.5	**45.5**	48	**50.5**	in

LENGTH TO UNDERARM

45	**45**	45	**46**	46	**48**	48	**48**	48	**48**	cm
17.5	**17.5**	17.5	**18**	18	**19**	19	**19**	19	**19**	in

BACK NECK YOKE DEPTH

21	**21**	21	**22**	22	**23**	23	**23**	24	**24**	cm
8.25	**8.25**	8.5	**8.75**	8.75	**9**	9	**9**	9.25	**9.25**	in

FINISHED LENGTH

65	**65**	66	**68**	68	**71**	71	**71**	72	**72**	cm
25.75	**25.75**	26	**26.75**	26.75	**28**	28	**28**	28.25	**28.25**	in

SLEEVE LENGTH

43	**43**	43	**45**	45	**46**	46	**46**	48	**48**	cm
17	**17**	17	**17.5**	17.5	**18**	18	**18**	19	**19**	in

HIP

81	**86**	91	**97**	102	**107**	112	**117**	122	**127**	cm
32	**34**	36	**38**	40	**42**	44	**46**	48	**50**	in

WAIST

68	**73**	78	**84**	89	**94**	99	**104**	109	**114**	cm
27	**29**	31	**33**	35	**37**	39	**41**	43	**45**	in

MATERIALS

Jamieson & Smith 2 Ply Jumper Weight (100% Shetland Wool; 118m/25g balls)

MC: SHADE 77
8 (**9**, 9, **10**, 11, **12**, 12, **13**, 13, **14**) x 25g balls

CC1: SHADE 142
1 x 25g ball all sizes

CC2: SHADE 9097
1 x 25g ball all sizes

CC3: SHADE 125
1 x 25g ball all sizes

CC4: SHADE 91
1 x 25g ball all sizes

CC5: SHADE 28
1 x 25g ball all sizes

CC6: SHADE 202
1 (**1**, 1, **1**, 1, **2**, 2, **2**, 2, **2**) x 25g balls

3mm (UK 11/US 2-3) circular needles (or size to get gauge) in the following lengths:
1 x 60cm/24in long; 1 x 100cm/40in long (for working yoke and neck); 1 x 20cm long (for sleeves, or use your preferred needles for working small diameters in the round)

2.75mm (UK 12/US 2) circular needles in the following length:
1 x 60cm/ 24in (for working rib)

Waste yarn or stitch holders
Stitch markers
Tapestry needle for weaving in ends

TENSION
Work two tension swatches as follows:

Chevron pattern
Cast on 57 sts with MC, pm and join for working in the round.
Round 1: Reading from right to left, work from row 1 of chart (or written instructions from step 6 below), repeating motif 3 times in total.
Last round sets pattern. Cont to work in pattern as set until row 16 is complete. Work rows 1-16 twice more.
Bind off. Block your swatch and count the number of sts and rounds to 10cm/4in.

28 sts and 36 rounds to 10cm/4in over garter st chevron pattern using 3mm needles

Stocking stitch
Cast on 40 sts with CC6 (It is easier to count the number of sts in a swatch knitted in CC6 than in MC), pm and join for working in the round.
Round 1: K to end.
Repeat last round 39 more times.
Bind off. Block your swatch and count the number of sts and rounds to 10cm/4in.

28 sts and 36 rounds to 10cm/4in over single-shade stocking st using 3mm needles

You must match the correct tension in both stitch patterns, or your sweater will not fit. If you have too many sts to 10cm/4in, then you need to use a larger needle. If you have too few sts to 10cm/4in, then you need to use a smaller needle. In either case you will need to prepare a new tension swatch as described above. Getting the correct tension in one stitch pattern does not guarantee matching tension in a different stitch pattern.

ABBREVIATIONS
See full list of abbreviations on page 87.

INSTRUCTIONS

1

CAST ON, WORK RIB, PLACE SIDE MARKERS

With MC and 2.75mm circular needle (60cm/24in long), cast on 224 (**238**, 252, **266**, 280, **294**, 308, **322**, 336, **350**) sts, pm, and join for working in the round.
Round 1: *K1, p1* repeat from * to * to end.
Last round sets 1x1 rib. Work in 1x1 rib for 26 more rounds.

Change to 3mm needles.
Round 28: K112 (**119**, 126, **133**, 140, **147**, 154, **161**, 168, **175**) sts, pm, k to end of round (markers now set position of side shaping).

2

WORK WAIST SHAPING, COMPLETE BODY

A: K1, k2tog, k to 3 sts before next marker, ssk, k1, slm, k1, k2tog, k to last 3 sts, ssk, k1.
B: K 6 rounds.
Repeat steps A and B 8 more times. 188 (**202**, 216, **230**, 244, **258**, 272, **286**, 300, **314**) sts.

K 9 rounds. (Consult schematic: if you wish to add length, do so here.)

A: K1, m1, k to 1 st before next marker, m1, k1, slm, k1, m1, k to last st, m1, k1.
B: K 6 rounds.
Repeat steps A and B 7 (7, 6, **7**, 6, **7**, 7, **7**, 8, **9**) more times. 220 (**234**, 244, **262**, 272, **290**, 304, **318**, 336, **354**) sts.

Work straight for 2 (**2**, 9, **6**, 13, **15**, 15, **15**, 8, **1**) more rounds. Piece should measure 45 (**45**, 45, **46**, 46, **48**, 48, **48**, 48, **48**) cm/17.5 (**17.5**, 17.5, **18**, 18, **19**, 19, **19**, 19, **19**) in from cast-on edge.

3

SET ASIDE STS AT UNDERARM

Moving sts around needles without knitting, slip 6 (**7**, 7, **7**, 7, **8**, 8, **8**, 9, **10**) sts each side of each marker to waste yarn. Two sets of 12 (**14**, 14, **14**, 14, **16**, 16, **16**, 18, **20**) sts set aside for underarms and two sets of 98 (**103**, 108, **117**, 122, **129**, 136, **143**, 150, **157**) sts for front/back remain.
Set body aside.

4

MAKE SLEEVES

With MC and 2.75mm needle (20cm long, or your preferred needles for working small circumferences in the round), cast on 52 (**54**, 58, **60**, 60, **62**, 62, **64**, 66, **70**) sts, pm and join for working in the round.
Work in 1x1 rib, as set on body, for 27 rounds.

Change to 3mm needles.
K 3 rounds.

A: K1, m1, k to last st, m1, k1.
B: K 4 (**4**, 4, **4**, 3, **3**, 3, **3**, 3, **3**) rounds.
Repeat steps A and B 20 (**22**, 22, **23**, 24, **26**, 26, **27**, 28, **28**) more times. 94 (**100**, 104, **108**, 110, **116**, 116, **120**, 124, **128**) sts.

K all rounds until sleeve measures 43 (**43**, 43, **45**, 45, **46**, 46, **46**, 48, **48**) cm/17 (**17**, 17, **17.5**, 17.5, **18**, 18, **18**, 19, **19**) in (or desired length to underarm).

Moving sts around needles without knitting, slip 6 (**7**, 7, **7**, 7, **8**, 8, **8**, 9, **10**) sts each side of marker to waste yarn. 12 (**14**, 14, **14**, 14, **16**, 16, **16**, 18, **20**) sts set aside at underarm and 82 (**86**, 90, **94**, 96, **100**, 100, **104**, 106, **108**) sts remain.
Set aside. Make another sleeve in the same way.

5

JOIN SLEEVES AND BODY INTO YOKE, ADJUST ST COUNT, PREPARE FOR CHART

Without knitting, slip first 49 (**52**, 54, **59**, 61, **65**, 68, **72**, 75, **79**) body sts around needles, so that you are in the centre of one section of sts (front/back are identical to this point, the chosen section is now the back).

With MC, RS facing and 3mm circular needle (100cm/40in long), and **purling every st**, join body and sleeves to yoke as follows:
P49 (**51**, 54, **58**, 61, **64**, 68, **71**, 75, **78**) sts of back, pm, p82 (**86**, 90, **94**, 96, **100**, 100, **104**, 106, **108**) sts of left sleeve, pm, p98 (**103**, 108, **117**, 122, **129**, 136, **143**, 150, **157**) sts of front, pm, p82 (**86**, 90, **94**, 96, **100**, 100, **104**, 106, **108**) sts of right sleeve, pm, p49 (**52**, 54, **59**, 61, **65**, 68, **72**, 75, **79**) sts rem from back and pm for new start of round. 360 (**378**, 396, **422**, 436, **458**, 472, **494**, 512, **530**) sts.

First to third, fifth, seventh, ninth and tenth sizes only
Next round (inc): K to marker, m1, slm, k to next marker, [m1] 0 (**0**, 1, -, 0, -, 1, -, 0, **0**) time, slm, knit to next marker, [m1] 0 (**1**, 1, -, 0, -, 1, -, 0, **1**) time, slm, knit to end, slipping last marker. 361 (**380**, 399, -, 437, -, 475, -, 513, **532**) sts.

Fourth and sixth sizes only
Next round (dec): K to marker, slm, k2tog, k to next marker, slm, [k2tog] - (-, -, **1**, -, **0**, -, -, -, -) time, k to next marker, slm, [k2tog] - (-, -, **1**, -, 0, -, -, -, -) time, k to next marker, slm, k2tog, k to end. - (-, -, **418**, -, **456**, -, -, -, -) sts.

Eighth size only
Next round: K to end.

All sizes
Remove all markers except start of round marker (at centre of back). Starting with a purl round, work 1 (**1**, 3, **3**, 3, **5**, 5, **5**, 7, **7**) rounds in garter st (p 1 round, k 1 round), thus ending with a p round.

6

PLACE MARKERS, WORK CHEVRON PATTERN

Work from either charted or written instructions as follows:

Working from chart (see below for written instructions)
Round 1: Reading from right to left, work row 1 of chart, repeating motif 19 (**20**, 21, **22**, 23, **24**, 25, **26**, 27, **28**) times in total and placing a marker every 19 sts to separate pattern repeats.
Round 2: Reading from right to left, work row 2 of chart, repeating motif 19 (**20**, 21, **22**, 23, **24**, 25, **26**, 27, **28**) times in total and slipping markers.
These two rounds set the chart pattern. Cont to work from chart until row 50 is complete.
Stitch counts at end of decrease rounds are as foll:
Round 17: 323 (**340**, 357, **374**, 391, **408**, 425, **442**, 459, **476**) sts.
Round 21: 285 (**300**, 315, **330**, 345, **360**, 375, **390**, 405, **420**) sts.
Round 33: 247 (**260**, 273, **286**, 299, **312**, 325, **338**, 351, **364**) sts.
Round 37: 209 (**220**, 231, **242**, 253, **264**, 275, **286**, 297, **308**) sts.
Round 43: 171 (**180**, 189, **198**, 207, **216**, 225, **234**, 243, **252**) sts.
Round 49: 133 (**140**, 147, **154**, 161, **168**, 175, **182**, 189, **196**) sts.

Working from written instructions (see above for charted instructions)

Round 1: With MC, *kfb, k7, sl2 knitwise, k1, p2sso, k7, kfb, pm* repeat from * to * to end.

Round 2 and all foll even-numbered rounds: With same shade as previous round, p to end.

Round 3: With CC1, *kfb, k7, sl2 knitwise, k1, p2sso, k7, kfb, slm* repeat from * to * to end.

Round 5: With CC2, as round 3.

Round 7: With CC3, as round 3.

Round 9: With CC4, as round 3.

Round 11: With CC5, as round 3.

Rounds 13 and 15: With CC6, as round 3.

Round 17: With MC, *kfb, k5, ssk, sl2 knitwise, k1, p2sso, k2tog, k5, kfb, slm* repeat from * to * to end. 323 (**340**, 357, **374**, 391, **408**, 425, **442**, 459, **476**) sts.

Round 19: With CC1, *kfb, k6, sl2 knitwise, k1, p2sso, k6, kfb, slm* repeat from * to * to end.

Round 21: With CC2, *kfb, k4, ssk, sl2 knitwise, k1, p2sso, k2tog, k4, kfb, slm* repeat from * to * to end. 285 (**300**, 315, **330**, 345, **360**, 375, **390**, 405, **420**) sts.

Round 23: With CC3, *kfb, k5, sl2 knitwise, k1, p2sso, k5, kfb, slm* repeat from * to * to end.

Round 25: With CC4, as round 23.

Round 27: With CC5, as round 23.

Rounds 29 and 31: With CC6, as round 23.

Round 33: With MC, *kfb, k3, ssk, sl2 knitwise, k1, p2sso, k2tog, k3, kfb, slm* repeat from * to * to end. 247 (**260**, 273, **286**, 299, **312**, 325, **338**, 351, **364**) sts.

Round 35: With CC1, *kfb, k4, sl2 knitwise, k1, p2sso, k4, kfb, slm* repeat from * to * to end.

Round 37: With CC2, *kfb, k2, ssk, sl2 knitwise, k1, p2sso, k2tog, k2, kfb, slm* repeat from * to * to end. 209 (**220**, 231, **242**, 253, **264**, 275, **286**, 297, **308**) sts.

Round 39: With CC3, *kfb, k3, sl2 knitwise, k1, p2sso, k3, kfb, slm* repeat from * to * to end.

Round 41: With CC4, as round 39.

Round 43: With CC5, *kfb, k1, ssk, sl2 knitwise, k1, p2sso, k2tog, k1, kfb, slm* repeat from * to * to end. 171 (**180**, 189, **198**, 207, **216**, 225, **234**, 243, **252**) sts.

Round 45: With CC6, *kfb, k2, sl2 knitwise, k1, p2sso, k2, kfb, slm* repeat from * to * to end.

Round 47: As round 45.

Round 49: With MC, *kfb, ssk, sl2 knitwise, k1, p2sso, k2tog, kfb, slm* repeat from * to * to end. 133 (**140**, 147, **154**, 161, **168**, 175, **182**, 189, **196**) sts.

Round 50: With MC, p to end.

7

COMPLETE YOKE, WORK SHORT ROW SHAPING

Next round (dec): With MC, k0 (**4**, 12, **2**, 7, **6**, 10, **6**, 15, **16**), *k2tog, k131 (**15**, 7, **36**, 12, **7**, 9, **6**, 4, **3**)* repeat from * to * to end. 132 (**132**, 132, **150**, 150, **150**, 160, **160**, 160, 160) sts.
Next round: P to end.

Before beginning next step, familiarise yourself with the instructions for short rows in the **Special Techniques** section on page 84.

Sizes are listed in the table from left to right. Select the relevant column for your size, then work as follows.
Short row 1 (RS): Beginning at start of round, knit the number of sts in first row for your size, then turn.
Short row 2 (WS): Knit the number of sts in the second row for your size, turn.
Last 2 rows set garter st short rows. Cont to work short rows from table as set, until all rows for your size are complete.

Next round (partial): K to end of round marker, closing gaps of all short rows.
Next round: K a complete round, closing gaps of all short rows.
Next round: P to end.

SHORT ROW SHAPING

	FIRST	**SECOND**	THIRD	**FOURTH**	FIFTH	**SIXTH**	SEVENTH	**EIGHTH**	NINTH	**TENTH**
ROW 1	40	**40**	40	**48**	48	**48**	50	**50**	50	**50**
ROW 2	80	**80**	80	**96**	96	**96**	100	**100**	100	**100**
ROW 3	77	**77**	77	**93**	93	**93**	97	**97**	97	**97**
ROW 4	74	**74**	74	**90**	90	**90**	94	**94**	94	**94**
ROW 5	71	**71**	71	**87**	87	**87**	91	**91**	91	**91**
ROW 6	68	**68**	68	**84**	84	**84**	88	**88**	88	**88**
ROW 7	none	**none**	none	**81**	81	**81**	85	**85**	85	**85**
ROW 8	none	**none**	none	**78**	78	**78**	82	**82**	82	**82**
ROW 9	none	**none**	none	**none**	none	**none**	none	**none**	79	**79**
ROW 10	none	**none**	none	**none**	none	**none**	none	**none**	76	**76**

8 WORK FINAL DECREASE ROUND, WORK RIB

First to third, seventh and eighth sizes only
Next round (dec): K1, *k2 (**2**, **2**, -, -, -, 1, **1**, -, -),
k2tog* repeat from * to * to last 3 (**3**, **3**, -, -, -, 3,
3, -, -) sts, k to end. 100 (**100**, 100, -, -, -, 108,
108, -, -) sts.

Fourth to sixth, ninth and tenth sizes only
Next round (dec): *[K1, k2tog] - (-, -, **17**, 3, **3**, -,
-, 2, **2**) times, [k2, k2tog] - (-, -, **6**, 4, **4**, -, -, 1, **1**)
time* repeat from * to * - (-, -, **1**, 5, **5**, -, -, 15, **15**)
more times. - (-, -, **104**, 108, **108**, -, -, 112, **112**) sts.

All sizes
Change to 2.75mm needles and work in 1x1 rib,
as set on body, for 10 rounds.
Bind off all sts using your favourite stretchy bind-
off method (see **Special Techniques**, page 84).

9 FINISHING

Graft sts at underarms together using Kitchener
Stitch. Weave in all ends to the back of the work.
Soak garment in tepid water with wool wash to
allow the sts to relax and bloom. Rinse carefully

in cold water. Press garment between towels
to remove water. Shape garment to correct
dimensions and pin out flat, or dry over dress
form. Leave to dry completely.

Enjoy your Puffin Sweater!

CHART (PUFFIN SWEATER)

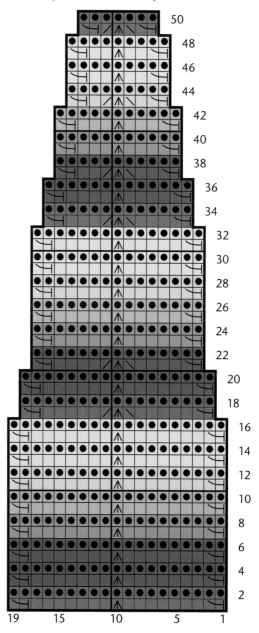

KEY

▨ MC (77); Knit

▨ CC1 (142); Knit

▨ CC2 (9097); Knit

▨ CC3 (125); Knit

▨ CC4 (91); Knit

▨ CC5 (28); Knit

☐ CC6 (202); Knit

Ⱉ Using shade as indicated;
sl2 sts knitwise, k1, p2sso

◥ Using shade as indicated; ssk

◿ Using shade as indicated; k2tog

⊞ Using shade as indicated; kfb

● Using shade as indicated; purl

PUFFIN MANTLE

A short wrap with a colourful and striking puffin-beak pattern.

SIZE
One size only
Circumference at lower edge: 138cm/54.25in
Depth at front: 24cm/9.5in
The circumference can easily be adjusted, if required, by adding or removing multiples of the 19-st pattern repeat. Don't forget that you will need to adjust your yarn quantities to reflect any changes.

MATERIALS
Jamieson & Smith 2 Ply Jumper Weight (100% Shetland Wool; 118m/25g balls)

MC:	**SHADE 77** 1 x 25g balls	**CC4:**	**SHADE 91** 1 x 25g balls
CC1:	**SHADE 142** 1 x 25g balls	**CC5:**	**SHADE 28** 1 x 25g balls
CC2:	**SHADE 9097** 1 x 25g balls	**CC6:**	**SHADE 202** 1 x 25g balls
CC3:	**SHADE 125** 1 x 25g balls		

3mm (UK 11/US 2-3) circular needle (or size to get gauge) in the following length:
1 x 60cm/24in long
Stitch markers
Tapestry needle for weaving in ends

TENSION
Chevron pattern
Cast on 57 sts with MC, pm and join for working in the round.
Round 1: Reading from right to left, work from row 1 of chart (or written instructions from step 1 below), repeating motif 3 times in total.
Last round sets pattern. Cont to work in pattern as set until row 16 is complete. Work rows 1-16 twice more.
Bind off. Block your swatch and count the number of sts and rounds to 10cm/4in.

28 sts and 36 rounds to 10cm/4in over garter st chevron pattern using 3mm needles

ABBREVIATIONS
See full list of abbreviations on page 87.

INSTRUCTIONS

1

CAST ON, START CHART PATTERN
With MC and 3mm needle, use the long-tail method to cast on 380 sts, pm, and join for working in the round.

Set-up round: P to end.

Work from either charted or written instructions as follows:
Working from chart (see below for written instructions)
Round 1: Reading from right to left, work from row 1 of chart, repeating motif 20 times in total. Last round sets chart pattern. Continue to work in pattern until chart row 82 is complete, then move to step 2 below.
Stitch counts at end of decrease rounds are as foll:
Round 17: 340 sts.
Round 33: 300 sts.
Round 49: 260 sts.
Round 65: 220 sts.

Working from written instructions (see above for charted instructions)
Round 1: With MC, *kfb, k7, sl2 knitwise, k1, p2sso, k7, kfb, pm* repeat from * to * to end.
Round 2 and all foll even-numbered rounds: With same shade as previous round, p to end.
Round 3: With CC1, *kfb, k7, sl2 knitwise, k1, p2sso, k7, kfb, slm* repeat from * to * to end.
Round 5: With CC2, as round 3.
Round 7: With CC3, as round 3.
Round 9: With CC4, as round 3.
Round 11: With CC5, as round 3.
Rounds 13 and 15: With CC6, as round 3.
Round 17: With MC, *kfb, k5, ssk, sl2 knitwise, k1, p2sso, k2tog, k5, kfb, slm* repeat from * to * to end. 340 sts.
Round 19: With CC1, *kfb, k6, sl2 knitwise, k1, p2sso, k6, kfb, slm* repeat from * to * to end.
Round 21: With CC2, as round 19.
Round 23: With CC3, as round 19.
Round 25: With CC4, as round 19.
Round 27: With CC5, as round 19.
Rounds 29 and 31: With CC6, as round 19.

Round 33: With MC, *kfb, k4, ssk, sl2 knitwise, k1, p2sso, k2tog, k4, kfb, slm* repeat from * to * to end. 300 sts.

Round 35: With CC1, *kfb, k5, sl2 knitwise, k1, p2sso, k5, kfb, slm* repeat from * to * to end.

Round 37: With CC2, as round 35.

Round 39: With CC3, as round 35.

Round 41: With CC4, as round 35.

Round 43: With CC5, as round 35.

Rounds 45 and 47: With CC6, as round 35.

Round 49: With MC, *kfb, k3, ssk, sl2 knitwise, k1, p2sso, k2tog, k3, kfb, slm* repeat from * to * to end. 260 sts.

Round 51: With CC1,*kfb, k4, sl2 knitwise, k1, p2sso, k4, kfb, slm* repeat from * to * to end.

Round 53: With CC2, as round 51.

Round 55: With CC3, as round 51.

Round 57: With CC4, as round 51.

Round 59: With CC5, as round 51.

Rounds 61 and 63: With CC6, as round 51.

Round 65: With MC, *kfb, k2, ssk, sl2 knitwise, k1, p2sso, k2tog, k2, kfb, slm* repeat from * to * to end. 220 sts.

Round 67: With CC1, *kfb, k3, sl2 knitwise, k1, p2sso, k3, kfb, slm* repeat from * to * to end.

Round 69: With CC2, as round 67.

Round 71: With CC3, as round 67.

Round 73: With CC4, as round 67.

Round 75: With CC5, as round 67.

Rounds 77 and 79: With CC6, as round 67.

Round 81: With MC, as round 67.

Round 82: With MC, p to end.

KEY

- ■ MC (77); Knit
- ■ CC1 (142); Knit
- ■ CC2 (9097); Knit
- ■ CC3 (125); Knit
- ■ CC4 (91); Knit
- ■ CC5 (28); Knit
- □ CC6 (202); Knit
- Ⓐ Using shade as indicated; Sl2 sts knitwise, k1, p2sso
- ◺ Using shade as indicated; ssk
- ◿ Using shade as indicated; k2tog
- ⊢ Using shade as indicated; kfb
- ● Using shade as indicated; purl

2

WORK SHORT ROW SHAPING

Before beginning next step, familiarise yourself with the instructions for short rows in the Special Techniques section, page 84.

As you will now be working back and forth, you will knit all rows to maintain garter st. With MC only, work as follows:

Short row 1 (RS): K55, turn.

Short row 2 (WS): K110, turn.

Short row 3: K105, turn.

Short row 4: K100, turn.

Short row 5: K95, turn.

Short row 6: K90, turn.

Short row 7: K88, turn.

Short row 8: K86, turn.

Now return to working in the round as follows:

Next round (partial): K to end of round marker, closing gaps of all short rows.

Next round: K a complete round, closing gaps of all short rows.

Next round: P to end. With MC, bind off all sts.

3

FINISHING

Weave in all ends to the back of the work. Soak garment in tepid water with wool wash to allow the sts to relax and bloom. Rinse carefully in cold water. Press between towels to remove water. Shape garment to correct dimensions and pin out flat. Leave to dry completely.

Enjoy your Puffin Mantle!

Reading Ursula Venables

We meet the engaging writer, naturalist and craftswoman, for whom Shetland's wild midsummer landscape held a unique charm.

I've read many books about Shetland, but there are few that I've enjoyed more than those by Ursula Venables. This now little-known naturalist and writer grew up in Pembrokeshire and was educated at Oxford University, where she later went on to teach Zoology. It was at Oxford that she met fellow naturalist, Llewellyn Sidney Vaugham Venables, (sensibly known to all his friends as 'Pat').

In the early 1930s, Pat had made several happy trips to Shetland in order to investigate its bird life, and was determined to return. After the dark and difficult years of the Second World War, in 1946, an opportunity arose, and the Venables upped sticks and moved to Shetland. They lived there for eight years, first at Whiteness and later near Spiggie Loch, where they purchased croft and tenure. The Venables' time in Shetland resulted in the first systematic zoological study of its fauna, *Birds and Mammals of Shetland* (1955), a book dedicated to their Shetland friends and whose findings still remain significant today. But while *Birds and Mammals* is an important book, it is perhaps Ursula's two memoirs, drawn from the diaries she kept while living in Shetland, that make the better read. These books provide intriguing and engaging accounts of life in post-war Shetland, and of a 'greenhorn' (as Ursula describes herself) getting to grips with new *modes* and *mores*.

TEMPESTUOUS EDEN

Ursula's first memoir is called *Tempestuous Eden* (1952) and it is a fitting title. For even the biblical Eden was no wild paradise, but a *garden*: a cultivated space defined by human labour. Similarly, Shetland for the Venables was not (as it sometimes seems for other Nineteenth- and Twentieth-Century English writers) a place of escape, surrounded by notions of romance, but was a primarily a location for their research. The Venables were in Shetland to work, and they worked extremely hard.

Ursula's memoirs suggest that she and Pat were more often than not outside, cycling and walking for miles in all weathers, their hardiness and doggedness in pursuit of their observations drawing the consternation (and sometimes admiration) of their friends and neighbours.

Without making any sort of fuss about it, the Venables became crofters as well as academics. They cared for livestock, grew crops and maintained land, boats and buildings.

Their own studies of Shetland's bird-life took time, care and lots of energy, and the Venables were often seconded to conduct other's research as well:

> As a pair of reasonably efficient people in an out of the way place, we were constantly being asked to perform small labours for scientists in the South. The Hope Department at Oxford wanted a selection of Shetland beetles, the Plymouth marine laboratory would like specimens of Gammarus, someone at Rothampstead wanted fresh rabbits' ears for ectoparasites, someone else wanted fulmar's gonads; there were regular counts to be made for the International Wildfowl Inquiry and regular abstracts to be written for the Ibis.

CYLINDERS AND PLANES

The Venables' certainly had their hands full and not just with research. Without making any sort of fuss about it, they became crofters as well as academics. They cared for livestock, grew crops and maintained land, boats, and buildings. Several chapters explore the back-breaking activity of cutting, hauling and drying peat – work which neither of the Venables particularly enjoyed, but definitely appreciated when the dark and cold of winter nights was warmed by the glow of their peat fire.

Ursula clearly enjoyed the company of her neighbours, and became passionately interested in Shetland crafts. She rooed[1] sheep, spun wool and knitted, and soon developed a knack for working Fair Isle. She was also a keen advocate of local knitting methods:

> Most garments are knitted in circular fashion, as we would knit a sock. [Shetland] very reasonably accepts the human body as cylindrical, whereas Paris regards it as a plane adorned here and there with emphatic bulges.

With varying degrees of success, she also experimented with natural dyes, including several recipes for dyeing with Shetland plants and lichens in her second memoir, *Life in Shetland* (1956). While Ursula was clearly a can-do person, game for pretty much anything, her efforts to produce blue yarn with powdered indigo and urine gathered from a Lerwick pub were never to be repeated. 'I felt,' she wrote 'like a body snatcher who had exhumed a thoroughly unpleasant corpse and had only himself to blame.'

AN ARDENT SUMMER LIFE

While Ursula clearly enjoyed most aspects of 'Life in Shetland', it is when writing about the landscape that her writing really springs to life. She loved the islands' breathtaking views, their shifting colours, their intensity, their drama. In summer, the landscape seems to take hold of her prose and runs away with it. 'For who would choose,' she asks, 'to stay indoors when immediately outside the seas were spreading their carpet of

[1] roo = removing fleece from the sheep by hand-plucking the wool

foam, and new flowers lighting up for the daily festival?' Venables had a particular fondness for Shetland's wildflowers, describing how they emerged in turn to transform the landscape, and make it their own.

In May [spring scilla] lay like a mist of spring rain between you and the green earth, in such widespread abundance that I always think of them as Shetland's national flower... In June, the moss campion was in full flower, masses of formal pink flowerets set in pincushions of brilliant green.

While Venables has a naturalist's eye for detail, she also has a way with the general scene. The feeling she conveys in the following paragraph will be familiar to anyone who has enjoyed a brisk walk on a beautiful June day to be rewarded with a spectacular Shetland panorama:

South from Havra, one could survey no less than twenty isles and holms in one wide view, stretching beyond the compass of the longest summer's day. They lay beneath the naked sky, unsung by man and rarely visited, sharing with the birds their ardent summer life, each a vivid world of light and colour and movement, enriched by the rhythms of sea and season. These islands have a healing power: the lilt and harmony of their life sweeps through our own, lifting the drab wrack of indifferent matters which settles about us.

DESIGNING URSULA

I read Ursula Venables' *Tempestuous Eden* one April and then took a trip to Shetland the following June. This was my first summer visit and I was totally bowled over by the beauty of the landscape at that heady time of year. The sense of air and space, and the unique quality of the light at midsummer is really quite incredible. Much like Ursula Venables, I felt compelled to spend all of my time outdoors. Over several happy days I wandered about the hills, cliffs and dunes, enjoying the wildflowers that illuminated the landscape in a shimmering haze of pink and blue.

After this summer visit, in which several aspects of Venables writing really struck home for me, I wanted to design a garment with a 1940s feel, the sort of thing that might well have been worn by Ursula herself when she lived in Shetland. Around the time that this idea occurred to me, I watched a BBC costume drama set in the immediate post-war period, in which a character was sporting precisely the sort of garment I had in mind. This on-screen cardigan featured a multi-coloured zigzagging pattern set over a plain fawn background. It made only a brief appearance in a single episode, but I committed its visual effect to memory and from that produced the Ursula chart. The shades I chose are those of Shetland's summer wildflowers: the pastel blue of spring squill and sheep's bit; the pale pink of moss campion and thrift; and the fresh, light green of sea rocket and sandwort.

While the chart is actually very straightforward and simple to knit, the Ursula Cardigan is probably the most technically challenging design in this collection (though I hope the instructions are clear enough for it to be tackled by any confident beginner). With its top-down set-in sleeves and clean finishing details, it is a structured, classic, feminine garment that should see the wearer through a good many Shetland summers.

The Ursula Mittens knit up very quickly, and would be a great way of assessing tension before taking on the larger project of the cardigan. Worn on the coldest days of winter, the mittens will remind you of midsummer days and walks to come.

RESOURCES

Ursula Venables, *Tempestuous Eden: The Story of A Naturalist in The Shetland Islands* (1952)
Ursula Venables and Llewellyn Sidney Vaugham Venables, *Birds and Mammals of Shetland* (1955)
Ursula Venables, *Life in Shetland* (1956)

PHOTOGRAPHY

32 Tombolo leading to St Ninian's Isle
33 Sea Campion
34 TOP   Sea campion (*Silene maritima*)
   MIDDLE   Spring squill (*Scilla verna*)
   BOTTOM Bog cotton (*Eriophorum angustifolium*)
35 TOP   Ursula Cardigan
   BOTTOM Shetland's luminous summer landscape
All images © Kate Davies Designs and www.shetland.org

URSULA CARDIGAN AND URSULA MITTENS

The shades of Shetland's summer wildflowers are reflected in the soft colours of this structured 1940s-inspired cardigan and warm mittens, which will keep your hands snug through the winter.

PATTERNS » CARDIGAN PAGE 38
MITTENS PAGE 48

SIZES

The fit of this garment is close, like the cardigans of the 1940s by which it is inspired; each size is factored with zero or *very slight* positive ease. I recommend choosing the size closest to your actual bust measurement or, if in doubt, the next size up.

TO FIT BUST

81	**86**	97	**102**	112	**122**	cm
32	**34**	38	**40**	44	**48**	in

ACTUAL BUST

81	**87**	97	**104**	114	**122**	cm
32	**34**	38.25	**41**	44.75	**48**	in

LENGTH TO UNDERARM

33	**35**	38	**40**	40	**41**	cm
13	**13.75**	15	**15.5**	15.75	**16.25**	in

ARMHOLE DEPTH

18	**19**	19	**20**	23	**24**	cm
7	**7.25**	7.5	**8**	9	**9.5**	in

FINISHED LENGTH

51	**54**	57	**60**	63	**65**	cm
20	**21**	22.75	**23.75**	24.5	**25.75**	in

SLEEVE LENGTH

38	**38**	39	**40**	42	**44**	cm
15	**15**	15.5	**15.75**	16.5	**17.25**	in

CROSS SHOULDERS

32	**35**	36	**38**	38	**41**	cm
12.75	**13.5**	14	**15**	15	**16**	in

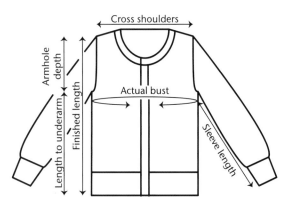

URSULA CARDIGAN

Cardigan with a pretty colourwork bodice and neat set-in sleeves, inspired by the hazy pinks and blues of Shetland's luminous summer landscape.

MATERIALS

Jamieson & Smith 2 Ply Jumper Weight (100% Shetland Wool; 118m/25g balls)

MC: SHADE **202**
10 (**12**, 13, **14**, 16, **18**) x 25g balls
CC1: SHADE FC24
2 (**2**, 2, **2**, 2, **3**) x 25g balls
CC2: SHADE 9144
2 (**2**, 2, **2**, 2, **3**) x 25g balls
CC3: SHADE FC15
2 (**2**, 2, **2**, 2, **3**) x 25g balls

LARGER NEEDLE

2.75	**3**	2.75	**3**	2.75	**3**	mm
12	**11**	12	**11**	12	**11**	UK
2	**2-3**	2	**2-3**	2	**2-3**	US

SMALLER NEEDLE

2.5	**2.75**	2.5	**2.75**	2.5	**2.75**	mm
13-12	**12**	13-12	**12**	13-12	**12**	UK
1-2	**2**	1-2	**2**	1-2	**2**	US

Larger circular needle (see table above) in the following length:
1 x 60cm/24in long
Smaller circular needle (see table above) in the following lengths:
1 x 60cm/24in long (for working rib); 1 x 80-100cm/30-40in long *or* dpns (for working sleeve caps)
2 x 2mm (UK 14/US 0) circular needle, any length (for picking up sts for sleeve caps)
Spare needles or waste yarn for holding stitches
Stitch markers

Tapestry needle for weaving in ends
Sewing needle
Six buttons
Six transparent button snaps (1-2cm/0.5in)
1m/1yd grosgrain ribbon or linen tape (3-4cm/
1-1.5in) wide for button band lining
Cotton sewing thread in similar shade to ribbon

TENSION

Work a tension swatch as follows:
Cast on 67 sts using larger needle, pm and join
for working in the round.
Round 1: Work first 7 sts from row 1 of chart A,
then work 5 repeats of the marked section from
row 1 of chart A.
Continue to work in pattern as set by last round,
until piece measures 15cm/6in.
Cast off all sts.
Reinforce and cut steek, following the instructions
in the **Special Techniques** section (page 84).
Block your swatch and count the sts and rounds
to 10cm/4in.

STITCHES TO 10CM/4IN

30	**28**	30	**28**	30	**28**

ROUNDS TO 10CM/4IN

38	**36**	38	**36**	38	**36**

You must match the correct tension **for your
size**, or your cardigan will not fit. If you have
too many sts to 10cm/4in, then you need to
use a larger needle. If you have too few sts to
10cm/4in, then you need to use a smaller needle.
In either case you will need to prepare a new
tension swatch as described above.

ABBREVIATIONS

See full list of abbreviations on page 87.

INSTRUCTIONS

1

CAST ON, SET UP CENTRE STEEK, WORK RIB

With MC, and smaller circular needle (60cm/24in
long), cast on 230 (**230**, 280, **280**, 330, **330**) sts,
pm, and join for working in the round.
Round 1: K7 (steek sts), pm, *k3, p2*, repeat
from * to * to last 3 sts, k3.
Last round sets 7 steek sts as stocking stitch and
3 x 2 rib on remaining sts.
Work as set for 6 (**6**, 9, **9**, 10, **10**) cm/2.5 (**2.5**,
3.5, **3.5**, 4, **4**) in.

2

INCREASE STS, PLACE SIDE MARKERS

Change to larger circular needle (60cm/24in
long). Continue to work with MC.
Next round (inc): K7 (steek sts), slm, k1, *k13
(**13**, 18, **18**, 25, **25**), m1*, repeat from * to *
15 (**15**, 13, **13**, 11, **11**) more times, k to end of
round. 16 (**16**, 14, **14**, 12, **12**) sts increased and
246 (**246**, 294, **294**, 342, **342**) sts total (includes
7 steek sts).
Next round: K7 (steek sts), slm, k59 (**59**, 71, **71**,
83, **83**) sts, pm (side marker), k121 (**121**, 145,
145, 169, **169**) sts, pm (side marker), k59 (**59**,
71, **71**, 83, **83**) sts to end of round.

3

BEGIN WORKING LOWER BODICE FROM CHART A

*In the following section, please ensure that you
are referring to the correct chart for your size.*
Round 1: Slipping markers as you come to
them, and reading all chart rows from right to
left, work first 7 (steek) sts from row 1 of chart
A, repeat marked section of chart A 19 (**19**, 23,
23, 27, **27**) times in total, work last 11 sts of
chart A once.
Last round sets chart A pattern. Cont to work
in patt as set until 33 (**33**, 36, **36**, 36, **36**) rows
of these charts have been completed 3 times.
99 (**99**, 108, **108**, 108, **108**) chart rounds
completed in total. If row tension is correct,
piece should measure 33 (**35**, 38, **40**, 40, **41**)
cm/13 (**13.75**, 15, **15.5**, 15.75, **16.25**) in from
cast-on edge.

4

SET ASIDE STS AT UNDERARMS, SET UP ARMHOLE
STEEKS, ESTABLISH UPPER BODICE CHARTS

Moving sts around needle without knitting, slip
7 (**7**, 8, **8**, 10, **10**) sts either side of each side
marker to waste yarn, removing markers. 14 (**14**,
16, **16**, 20, **20**) sts set aside for each underarm,
52 (**52**, 63, **63**, 73, **73**) sts for each front and 107
(**107**, 129, **129**, 149, **149**) sts for back remain.

Round 1: With MC only, k7 (steek sts), slm,
k52 (**52**, 63, **63**, 73, **73**), pm, using backward
loop method, cast on 7 armhole steek sts, pm,
k107 (**107**, 129, **129**, 149, **149**), pm, using
backward loop method, cast on 7 armhole
steek sts, pm, k52 (**52**, 63, **63**, 73, **73**) to end
of round. 232 (**232**, 276, **276**, 316, **316**) sts
(including 21 steek sts).

In the following section, please ensure you are referring to the correct chart for your size.

Round 2: Join in CC1, work 7 steek sts from row 2 chart B, slm, work across right front sts from row 2 chart C, decreasing as indicated, slm, work steek sts from row 2 chart D, slm, work across back sts from row 2 chart E, decreasing as indicated, slm, work steek sts from row 2 chart F, slm, work across left front sts from row 2 chart G, decreasing as indicated.

Last round sets positions for charts B, C, D, E, F and G. Continue to work from charts as set until row 22 (**22**, 24, **24**, 24, **24**) is complete. 208 (**208**, 228, **228**, 244, **244**) sts (including 21 steek sts). 46 (**46**, 51, **51**, 55, **55**) sts for each Front and 95 (**95**, 105, **105**, 113, **113**) sts for Back.

5 SET ASIDE FRONT NECK STS, RE-ESTABLISH FRONT STEEK

Round 23 (**23**, 25, **25**, 25, **25**): Using MC, bind off 7 sts (front steek), remove markers, and break yarn. Slip 12 sts from neck edges of left and right fronts to waste yarn (12 sts from each side of bound-off steek). Rejoining yarn to neck edge of left front, pm, cast on 7 sts using backward loop method, these are the front steek from chart B round 23 (**23**, 25, **25**, 25, **25**), continue working from chart C, round 23 (**23**, 25, **25**, 25, **25**), completing other charts in sequence as set. 184 (**184**, 204, **204**, 220, **220**) sts (including 21 steek sts).

6 COMPLETE UPPER BODICE

Following charts B-G in sequence, and working decreases as indicated, complete all charts to round 66 (**66**, 72, **72**, 85, **85**). 160 (**160**, 178, **178**, 194, **194**) sts (including 21 steek sts). 22 (**22**, 26, **26**, 30, **30**) sts for each Front and 95 (**95**, 105, **105**, 113, **113**) sts for Back.

7 BIND OFF STEEKS, SET ASIDE STS AT BACK NECK, GRAFT SHOULDERS

With MC only, and removing all markers when you encounter them, bind off 7 front steek sts, k until you have 22 (**22**, 26, **26**, 30, **30**) right front sts on needle after bound-off sts, bind off 7 armhole steek sts, k until you have 73 (**73**, 79, **79**, 83, **83**) back sts on needle after bound-off sts, then slip last 51 (**51**, 53, **53**, 53, **53**) sts just worked to

waste yarn for back neck, k22 (**22**, 26, **26**, 30, **30**) remaining sts of back, bind off 7 armhole steek sts, k until you have 22 (**22**, 26, **26**, 30, **30**) left front sts on needle after bound-off sts. Break yarn. 2 sets of 22 (**22**, 26, **26**, 30, **30**) sts remain for right shoulder, and 2 sets of 22 (**22**, 26, **26**, 30, **30**) sts remain for left shoulder. With RS facing outwards, graft together sts for right shoulder using Kitchener stitch. Repeat for left shoulder.

8 CUT STEEKS

Following instructions to reinforce and cut steeks from **Special Techniques** section (page 84), cut the steeks for front opening, followed by steeks for right and left armholes. With your iron on the wool setting, give the garment a light steam on the reverse to allow the sts to relax.

9 PICK UP STS FOR SLEEVE CAP

With MC and RS facing, using first 2mm circular needle, picking up sts in the gap between the end of steek and the beginning of pattern puk 6 (**6**, 8, **8**, 9, **9**) sts from underarm shaped rows, then puk 32 (**32**, 36, **36**, 40, **40**) sts up armhole to shoulder, pm, all sizes puk 1 st at top of shoulder, pm, puk 32 (**32**, 36, **36**, 40, **40**) sts down armhole, then puk 6 (**6**, 8, **8**, 9, **9**) sts in shaped rows. 77 (**77**, 89, **89**, 99, **99**) sts. Break yarn.

Using second 2mm needle, slip first 31 (**31**, 35, **35**, 38, **38**) picked-up sts to new needle, thus reaching 7 (**7**, 9, **9**, 11, **11**) sts before first marker at shoulder.

10 SHAPE SLEEVE CAP

Before beginning this step, read the instructions for 'Carol Sunday's short rows' in Special Techniques section, page 84.

From the RS, using smaller needles (circular or dpns), rejoin MC at point between needles, 7 (**7**, 9, **9**, 11, **11**) sts before first marker at shoulder.
Short row 1 (RS): K15 (**15**, 19, **19**, 23, **23**) sts across top of sleeve cap, removing both shoulder markers, and turn.
Short row 2 (WS): P16 (**16**, 20, **20**, 24, **24**), turn.
Short row 3: K17 (**17**, 21, **21**, 25, **25**), turn.
Short row 4: P18 (**18**, 22, **22**, 26, **26**), turn.
Continue in this manner, adding another st before each turn, until all the picked-up sts are incorporated into sleeve cap.

Last 2 short rows are as follows:
Next row (WS): P76 (**76**, 88, **88**, 98, **98**), turn.
Next row (RS): K77 (**77**, 89, **89**, 99, **99**). Do not turn.

Change to larger needles (circular or dpns) and knit across 7 (**7**, 8, **8**, 10, **10**) underarm sts held on waste yarn. Pm for new start of round.
Round 1: K7 (**7**, 8, **8**, 10, **10**) (rem underarm sts), and then k to end. 91 (**91**, 105, **105**, 119, **119**) sts.

Fifth and sixth sizes only
Next round: K2tog, k to end of round. 118 sts.

All sizes
K 6 rounds.

11 SHAPE SLEEVE

A: K1, k2tog, k to last 3 sts, ssk, k1.
B: K 5 (**4**, 4, **4**, 4, **4**) rounds.
Repeat steps A and B 17 (**17**, 19, **19**, 23, **23**) more times. 55 (**55**, 65, **65**, 70, **70**) sts.

K all rounds, without further shaping, until sleeve measures 32 (**32**, 33, **34**, 36, **38**) cm/12.5 (**12.5**, 13, **13.25**, 14, **14.75**) in from underarm (if you prefer a longer sleeve, work extra rounds here).

Next round: *K3, p2* rep from * to * to end of round.
Last round sets 3x2 rib. Work in 3x2 rib for 6cm/2.5in.
Bind off all stitches in rib.

Make another sleeve in the same way.

12 WORK BUTTON BANDS

With RS facing, using MC and smaller needle, picking up sts in the gap between end of steek and beginning of pattern, puk 88 (**88**, 98, **98**, 108, **108**) sts along right front edge opening.

Next row (WS): P3, *k2, p3* work from * to * to end of row.
Next row (RS): K3, *p2, k3* work from * to * to end of row.

Last 2 rows set 3x2 rib. Work in 3x2 rib as set for another 9 (**9**, 13, **13**, 13, **13**) rows. Bind off all sts in rib. Work the left button band in the same way.

13 WORK NECK EDGING

With RS facing, using MC and smaller circular needle, starting at neck edge of right front button band, puk 6 (**6**, 8, **8**, 8, **8**) sts across top of right front button band, knit across 12 sts from waste yarn, puk between steek and pattern sts 31 (**31**, 33, **33**, 38, **38**) sts up right front neck, puk 2 sts at right shoulder, knit across 51 (**51**, 53, **53**, 53, **53**) sts from waste yarn at back neck, puk 2 sts at left shoulder, puk 31 (**31**, 33, **33**, 38, **38**) sts down left front neck, knit across 12 sts from waste yarn across top of left front button band, puk 6 (**6**, 8, **8**, 8, **8**) sts across top of right front button band. 153 (**153**, 163, **163**, 173, **173**) sts.

Next row (WS): P3, *k2, p3* repeat from * to * to end.
Next row (RS): K3, *p2, k3* repeat from * to * to end.
Last 2 rows set 3x2 rib. Work in 3x2 rib as set for 11 (**11**, 15, **15**, 15, **15**) rows. Bind off all sts in rib.

14 FINISHING

Weave in ends to the back of the work. Using back stitch and MC, lightly stitch down all steek edges to reverse of work. Soak garment in tepid water with wool wash to allow the sts to relax and bloom. Rinse carefully in cold water. Press garment between towels to remove water. Shape garment to correct dimensions and pin out flat. Leave to dry completely.
Measure your button bands carefully and cut your lining strip to these measurements, plus 1cm/0.5in (allowing space to turn the raw ends in and leave a scant 2-3mm/0.2in for stitching at top and bottom). Pin out lining strips, paying particular attention to the top and bottom of each strip, which should reach as closely as possible to the edges of the button bands. Now stitch lining strips in place using invisible slip stitch. Mark out positions for buttons and fasteners with pins. Sew the bottom of your fasteners in place along the front of the right button band. Sew the top of your fasteners in corresponding place along the underside of left button band. Sew your buttons in place along the top of left button band.

Enjoy your Ursula Cardigan!

URSULA CARDIGAN:
CHARTS FOR FIRST & SECOND SIZES

CHART G:
LEFT FRONT

CHART F:
STEEK

CHART E:
BACK (CONT)

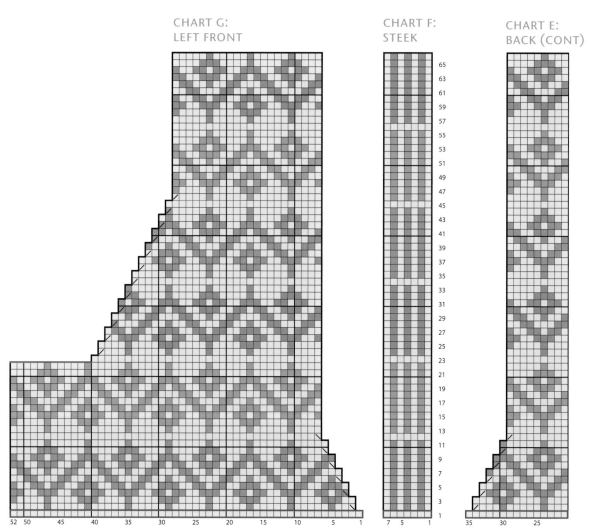

KEY

- ☐ MC (202); Knit
- ☐ CC1 (FC24); Knit
- ☐ CC2 (9144); Knit
- ☐ CC3 (FC15); Knit
- ☐ Pattern repeat
- ☐ See written instructions
- ◹ K2tog using shade as indicated
- ◺ Ssk using shade as indicated

CHART A:
BODY & STEEK

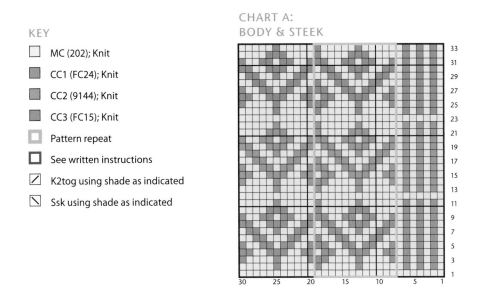

CHART E:
BACK

CHART D:
STEEK

CHART C:
RIGHT FRONT

CHART B:
STEEK

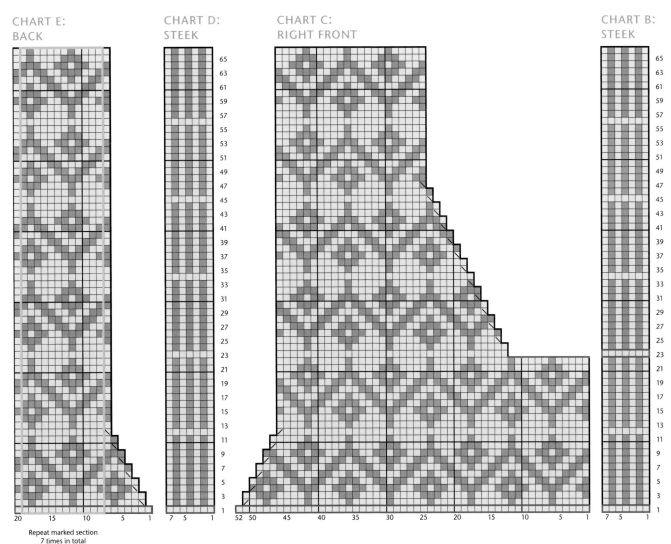

Repeat marked section
7 times in total

URSULA CARDIGAN:
CHARTS FOR THIRD & FOURTH SIZES

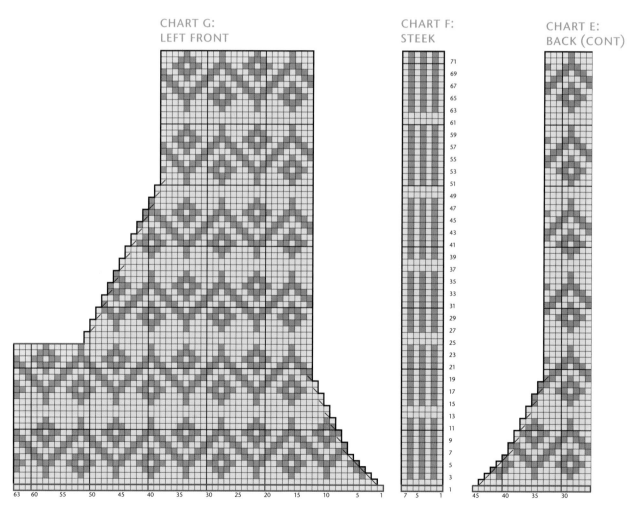

CHART G:
LEFT FRONT

CHART F:
STEEK

CHART E:
BACK (CONT)

KEY

- ☐ MC (202); Knit
- ☐ CC1 (FC24); Knit
- ☐ CC2 (9144); Knit
- ☐ CC3 (FC15); Knit
- ☐ Pattern repeat
- ☐ See written instructions
- ☑ K2tog using shade as indicated
- ☒ Ssk using shade as indicated

CHART A:
BODY & STEEK

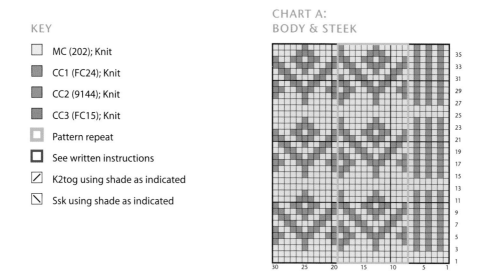

CHART E:
BACK

CHART D:
STEEK

CHART C:
RIGHT FRONT

CHART B:
STEEK

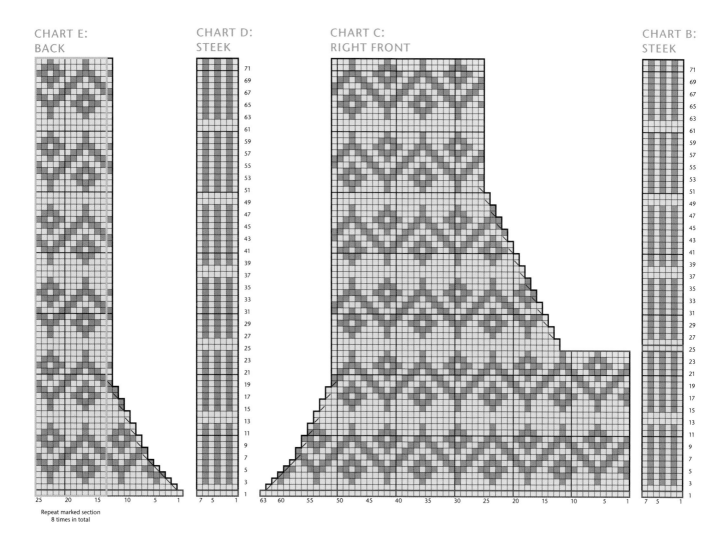

Repeat marked section
8 times in total

URSULA CARDIGAN:
CHARTS FOR FIFTH & SIXTH SIZES

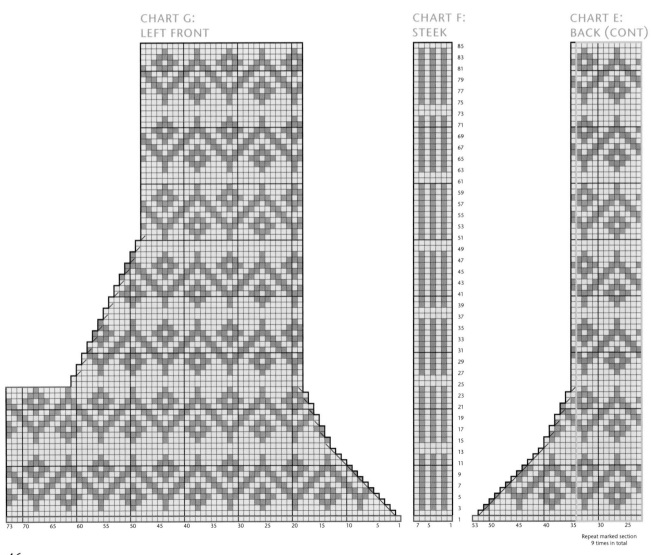

CHART G:
LEFT FRONT

CHART F:
STEEK

CHART E:
BACK (CONT)

Repeat marked section
9 times in total

KEY

- ☐ MC (202); Knit
- ■ CC1 (FC24); Knit
- ■ CC2 (9144); Knit
- ■ CC3 (FC15); Knit
- ☐ Pattern repeat
- ☐ See written instructions
- ◪ K2tog using shade as indicated
- ◩ Ssk using shade as indicated

CHART A: BODY & STEEK

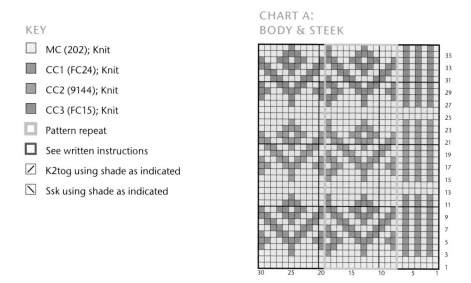

CHART E: BACK

CHART D: STEEK

CHART C: RIGHT FRONT

CHART B: STEEK

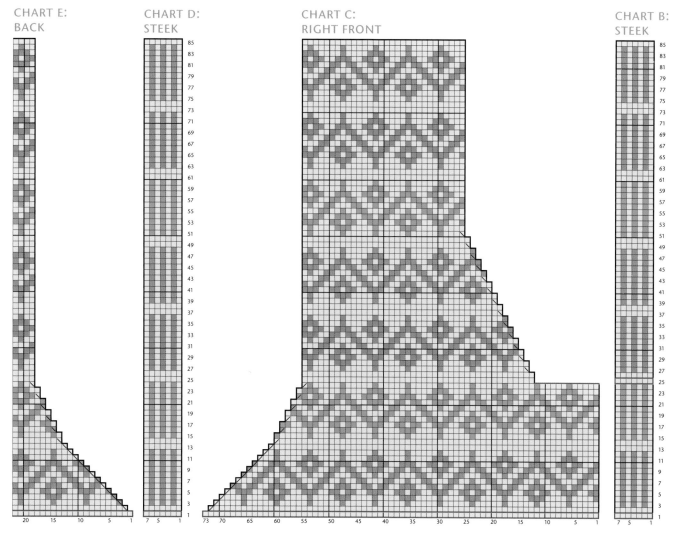

URSULA MITTENS

Pretty mittens in a soft, summery pattern to remind you of the warmer days to come.

SIZE

One size only
Hand circumference above thumb:
19cm/7.5in
Length: 23cm/9in
The hand circumference can be adjusted, if required, by adding or removing multiples of the 12-st pattern repeat. Don't forget that you will need to adjust your yarn quantities to reflect any changes.

MATERIALS

Jamieson & Smith 2 Ply Jumper Weight (100% Shetland Wool; 118m/25g balls)

MC: SHADE 202
2 x 25g balls
CC1: SHADE FC24
1 x 25g ball
CC2: SHADE 9144
1 x 25g ball
CC3: SHADE FC15
1 x 25g ball

2.5mm (UK 13/US 1) circular needle in the following length:
1 x 20cm/8in long or dpns
2.75mm (UK 12/US 2) circular needle in the following length:
1 x 20cm/8in long
2.75mm (UK 12/US 2) dpns (for thumb)
Stitch markers
Waste yarn (a smooth cotton 4 ply will work best as it won't stick to your main yarn)
Tapestry needle for weaving in ends

CHART

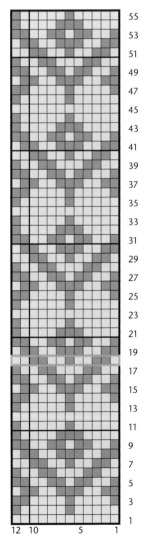

55
53
51
49
47
45
43
41
39
37
35
33
31
29
27
25
23
21
19
17
15
13
11
9
7
5
3
1

12 10   5   1

TENSION

Work a tension swatch as follows:
Cast on 48 sts using 2.75mm needles, pm and join for working in the round.
Round 1: Reading from right to left, work from row 1 of chart, repeating motif 4 times in total.
Last round sets chart pattern. Work in chart pattern until piece measures 13cm/5in.
Bind off all sts.

32 sts and 36 rounds to 10cm/4in over colourwork pattern using 2.75mm needles

You must match the correct tension, or your mittens will not fit. If you have too many sts to 10cm/4in, then you need to use a larger needle. If you have too few sts to 10cm/4in, then you need to use a smaller needle. In either case you will need to prepare a new tension swatch as described above.

ABBREVIATIONS

See full list of abbreviations on page 87.

KEY

☐ MC (202); Knit
■ CC1 (FC24); Knit
■ CC2 (9144); Knit
■ CC3 (FC15); Knit
☐ Thumb placement round

INSTRUCTIONS

1

CAST ON, ESTABLISH RIB

With CC3, and 2.5mm needles cast on 50 sts, pm, and join for working in the round.
Change to CC1.
Round 1: *K3, p2* repeat from * to * to end. Last round sets 3x2 rib.
Round 2: Change to CC2, and work in 3x2 rib as set.
Round 3: Change to MC, and work in 3x2 rib as set.
With MC, work in 3x2 rib for 17 more rounds.

Change to 2.75mm needles.

Round 21 (inc): *K5, m1* repeat from * to * to end. 60 sts.
Round 22: Reading from right to left, work from row 1 of chart, repeating motif 5 times in total. Last round sets chart pattern. Work until chart row 17 is complete.

2

THUMB PLACEMENT FOR RIGHT MITTEN

Next round: K1 in pattern from chart row 18, K9 using waste yarn, slip these 9 sts back onto left needle, and work to end of round in pattern from chart row 18.
You will now have 9 sts of waste yarn in your fabric. After completion of the hand, you will come back to these stitches, unpick the waste yarn, and work an 'afterthought' thumb.

3

COMPLETE CHART

Work chart rounds 19-55 as set.

4

SHAPE MITTEN TOP, GRAFT STS

Change to MC.
Next round: K30, pm, k to end of round. This marker and the existing start of round marker set position for decreases.
Next round (dec): *Slm, k1, ssk, k to 3 sts before next marker, k2tog, k1* repeat from * to * once more. 56 sts.
Repeat last round 10 more times. 16 sts.
Place first 8 sts of round and second 8 sts of round on 2 needles and hold parallel to each other. Graft these sts together using Kitchener stitch.

5

THUMB

With MC and 2.5mm dpn, pick up (but don't knit) 9 sts in row of sts below waste yarn. With second 2.5mm dpn, pick up (but don't knit) 9 sts in row of sts above waste yarn. Carefully remove waste yarn. Now join in yarn at start of lower needle, k9 from first dpn, pick up and knit 2 sts in gap between needles, k9 from second dpn, pick up and knit 2 sts in gap, pm for start of round. 22 sts. Redistribute sts on needles as desired.

With MC, k until thumb is 1cm/0.5in shorter than desired length (22 rounds will give an average thumb length).
Next round (dec): [K2tog] 11 times. 11 sts.
Next round: K to end.
Next round (dec): K2tog, k to end. 10 sts.
Next round: K to end.
Decrease round: [K2tog] 5 times. 5 sts.
Break yarn, and draw up tightly through remaining 5 sts.
Fasten off to inside of thumb.

6

LEFT HAND MITTEN

Work step 1 as for right mitten

7

THUMB PLACEMENT FOR LEFT MITTEN

Next round: Work 20 sts in pattern from chart row 18, K9 sts using waste yarn, slip these 9 sts back onto left needle, and work to end of round in pattern from chart row 18.
You will now have 9 sts of waste yarn in your fabric. After completion of the hand, you will come back to these stitches, unpick the waste yarn and work an 'afterthought' thumb.

8

COMPLETE LEFT MITTEN

Work steps 3 through 5 as for right mitten.

9

FINISHING

With tapestry needle, weave in all ends, paying particular attention to the thumb join which may need neatening. Soak mittens in tepid water and wool wash. Press between towels to remove water. Shape mittens to finished dimensions. Lie them flat and allow to dry fully.

Enjoy your Ursula Mittens!

Exploring Northmavine

Shetland possesses landscapes of great variety and contrast, and of nowhere is this more true than Northmavine.

Almost an island in itself, Northmavine is connected to the Shetland mainland by Mavis Grind – a narrow isthmus marking the meeting place of the North Sea and the Atlantic Ocean. Passing this crossroads on foot or by car, you can almost immediately sense the difference in the land. While the South Mainland has a gently rolling, almost domestic feel to it, in Northmavine, the surroundings are much more rocky and, perhaps, much more dramatic. If you enjoy a walk among wild hills and seascapes, there is really no place to beat it. From the rugged cliffs and arches of Eshaness to the majestic sweep of the Lang Ayre; from the glorious views of Fedaland, to the beautiful island of Uyea (which can be reached by foot at low tide) – Northmavine is truly breathtaking.

'AN IMMENSE, BARREN AND TRACKLESS WILDERNESS'

In 1817, Manchester polymath, Samuel Hibbert-Ware, travelled to Shetland to conduct a geological survey. Hibbert-Ware clearly enjoyed the challenges of Shetland's great outdoors and it is in the landscape of Northmavine that his prose really springs to life. He had a great observing eye and his account includes some memorable descriptions of the 'red barren scalp' of Ronas Hill, and the hearty 'mountain cheer' brought by a feast of cold Shetland lamb and Madeira at the end of a chilly walk. Here is one such moment when Hibbert-Ware, after ascending the burn of the 'Twa Roes', and leaving his companion fishing at Roer Water, tramps off to explore the landscape:

'We arrived in our ascent at an immense, barren and trackless wilderness, where the apparent disturbance, induced by the penetration of a mass of a large dike of greenstone, was exhibited in the deep hollows of a chain of lakes. In a southerly direction, the eye might trace the gradual ascent to the round summit of Ronas Hill, which was reflected into various tints and shades... Light wreathes of mist moved gently over the dreary waste, while the deepest silence prevailed, except when interrupted by the plaintive note of the plover, or the shrill cry of the whimbrel, whose haunts I had invaded. At length appeared in view a vast range of impendent cliffs, extending for a distance of ten miles, and worn by the action of a turbulent sea into a thousand fantastic forms. Insulated rocks were whitened with innumerable flocks of sea-fowl, and at their base were hollow caverns, the domicil of seals and otters. Some hundred feet below me, the billows of the Atlantic broke with tremendous roar...'

While the South Mainland has a gently rolling, almost domestic feel to it, in Northmavine, the surroundings are rockier and, perhaps, much more dramatic.

A FELSITE INTRUSION

The colours of my Northmavine designs are inspired by the forces that shape and define this landscape: the surprising teal of deep sea waves; the bright blue of a fast-moving sky against green hills; the swirling greys of the 'wreathes of mist' around Ronas Hill; and the unexpectedly subtle shades of what is referred to by Hibbert-Ware above as 'greenstone'. This 'greenstone' is, in fact, a rare form of felsite, occurring only in this part of Shetland, and immediately recognisable when you are out for a walk. The area rising above Collafirth to Ronas Hill and across the Beorgs of Uyea, is mostly composed of rugged granite boulder fields, and when one comes across a felsite intrusion, the contrast of its banded waves of greeny-blue against the surrounding reddish stone is powerful and striking.

There's plenty of evidence that Shetland's earliest human settlers found it striking too, since it is of this material that the mysterious neolithic 'knives' in the Shetland Museum are formed. These carefully polished and incredibly tactile objects are so beautiful and so well-preserved that their purpose is assumed to be ceremonial rather than functional. These 'knives' perfectly capture the landscape's striking green-blue aesthetic, celebrating the natural colours and beauty of its turbulent geology. You can still see evidence of these early neolithic excavations at the Beorgs of Uyea (*site marked on OS Explorer Map 469*).

Northmavine is a place where you really need warm clothing to wrap up against the weather, and it is for this explicit purpose that the two garments inspired by this landscape – a hap and a hoody – were designed.

HAPS AND HOODIES

As knitters, we may have come across the word 'hap' in reference to Shetland (or Shetland-type) shawls featuring simple openwork, but what precisely does it mean? 'Hap' is a word common to Scots and Northern English dialects, as well as Shetland, and means to wrap, to cover, or conceal. From the Fourteenth Century on, the word hap crops up frequently in a wide variety of northern texts, its usage ranging from the quotidian (the protection of crops in cold ground, the repair of a thatched roof) to the sombre (the wrapping of a corpse or the burying of a secret). In Scots, to be 'weel happit' means to be well wrapped-up against the cold, and it is perhaps in reference to colder winter weather that the word has been most often used.

In *The Brigs of Ayr* (1786), for example, Robert Burns summed up the time of year as 'when the stacks get on their winter haps', and James Hogg memorably captured the atmosphere of a chilly evening: 'When gloamin o'er the welkin steals / And haps the hills in sober grey' (*Forest Minstrel*, 1810). More recently, 'hap' appears as a singularly wintery covering in Edinburgh author James King Annand's lovely poem, *Purple Saxifrage* (1991).

> *Aneath a hap o snaw it derns*
> *Deep in a dwam for maist the year*
> *To burst throu in a bleeze o starns*
> *Syne skail its flourish on the stour.* [1]

When the weather is chilly, what better way to be 'weel happit' than in a warm and cosy wool shawl? While in nineteenth-century mainland Scotland, the noun 'hap' might suggest a plaid, maud or other type of women's wrap, in Shetland a 'hap' came specifically to refer to the attractive openwork coverings made and worn by the knitters of those islands. In contrast to the luxurious fine lace shawls that were produced for merchants or special occasions, haps were intended for everyday use, to be worn around the house or on the hill.

[1] *snaw = snow; derns = hides; dwam = dream; starns = stars; syne = then; skail = spill; stour = storm*

Spun and knitted thicker than fine lace, a hap was a garment with a function: to keep the body warm. Wrapped and tied around the torso, or tucked hood-like around the neck and chin, a good hap would efficiently insulate its Shetland wearer against the exigencies of cold and wind. Knitted over a background of garter stitch and featuring shaded chevrons of familiar Shetland openwork patterns (first in natural sheep-shades and later in dyed colours), haps could also be incredibly beautiful and striking in their simplicity. Like the best kind of functional clothing, haps possess a certain timelessness of design, and today this Shetland classic is frequently re-interpreted by knitters around the world.

In many ways, a hoody might be seen as a contemporary iteration of the hap – a cosy, functional covering in which to wrap yourself against the cold. While for centuries Western monks have sported cowls, and North Africans have worn Djelabas, the modern hoody really began life in upstate New York in the 1930s, as practical workwear for labourers in cold conditions. Rapidly achieving popularity with athletes throughout the '40s and '50s, it gained iconic status in 1976 as Rocky Balboa scaled the snowy steps of the Philadelphia Museum of Modern Art in a no-frills hoody of marl-grey.

Like the haps of Shetland women, the classic status of Rocky's grey hoody arises from its very celebration of ordinariness and functionality: haps and hoodies are both garments that are meant to be worked in; meant to be worn. So, whether you choose to make yourself a hap or a hoody in which to explore the magnificent landscape of Northmavine, may you be 'weel happit' in either.

RESOURCES
Peter Guy, *Walking the Coastline of Shetland, Number 4: Northmavine* (2006)
Samuel Hibbert, *A Description of the Shetland Islands Comprising an Account of their Geology, Scenery, Antiquities and Superstitions* (1822)
Tom Hubbard, ed, *The New Makars: Mercat Anthology of Contemporary Poetry in Scots* (1991)
Sharon Miller, *Shetland's Hap Shawls, Then and Now* (2006)
Shetland Museum, *Walking Shetland's Volcano* (2012)

PHOTOGRAPHY
50   View of Fedaland
51   Felsite knife in Shetland Museum
52   Northmavine hillside sign
53   RIGHT ABOVE AND BELOW:
      Northmavine Hap
      LEFT: Skerries off Fedaland
All images © Kate Davies Designs and www.shetland.org

NORTHMAVINE HOODY

Inspired by the storm greys, sea-greens and deep-blues of a landscape shaped by wind and water, the Northmavine Hoody features subtly shaded stripes and is finished with contrast facings and an i-cord bind-off.

PATTERN » PAGE 58

NORTHMAVINE HAP

Wrap up in this warm hap with its dramatic waves of colour echoing Northmavine's turbulent seascape.

PATTERN » PAGE 64

NORTHMAVINE HOODY

A classic hoody with subtly shaded stripes, inset pockets and neat turned facings.

SIZES

Northmavine is designed to fit neatly, and the pattern has been written with very slight positive ease.
If you would like the garment to fit as pictured, I recommend picking the size closest to your actual bust measurements. If you would like a looser, more casual fit, select the next size up.

TO FIT BUST

81	86	91	97	102	107	112	117	122	127	cm
32	34	36	38	40	42	44	46	48	50	in

ACTUAL BUST

81	87	91	97	103	109	113	119	125	129	cm
32	34.25	36	38.25	40.5	43	44.5	47	49	51	in

LENGTH TO UNDERARM

43	43	43	44	44	46	46	46	46	46	cm
17	17	17	17.5	17.5	18	18	18	18	18	in

ARMHOLE DEPTH

20	20	21	23	24	25	26	28	29	30	cm
8	8	8.5	9	9.5	10	10.5	11	11.5	12	in

FINISHED LENGTH

66	66	68	70	71	73	74	75	76	78	cm
26	26	26.5	27.5	28	29	29.25	29.5	30	30.5	in

SLEEVE LENGTH

43	43	43	44	44	46	46	46	47	48	cm
17	17	17	17.5	17.5	18	18	18	18.5	19	in

MATERIALS

Jamieson & Smith 2 Ply Jumper Weight (100% Shetland Wool; 118m/25g balls)

MC: SHADE 203
12 (**13**, 14, **15**, 16, **18**, 18, **19**, 21, **22**) x 25g balls

CC1: SHADE 141
2 (**3**, 3, **3**, 3, **3**, 4, 4, 4, **4**) x 25g balls

CC2: SHADE FC37
2 (**3**, 3, **3**, 3, **3**, 4, 4, 4, **4**) x 25g balls

CC3: SHADE 65
2 (**3**, 3, **3**, 3, **3**, 4, 4, 4, **4**) x 25g balls

CC4: SHADE FC41
2 (**3**, 3, **3**, 3, **3**, 4, 4, 4, **4**) x 25g balls

A small amount (less than 90m/100yds) of lining yarn for pockets. Sample used Orkney Angora 4 ply (100% angora; 400m/50g balls) in grey.

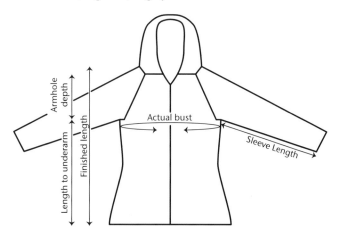

3mm (UK 11/US 2-3) circular needles (or size to get gauge) in the following lengths: 1 x 60cm/24in long; 3 x 80-100cm/30-40in long (for holding sts, working edging and finishing)
3.25mm (UK 10/US 3) dpns
3.25mm (UK 10/US D/3) crochet hook
Waste yarn (a smooth cotton 4 ply will work best as it won't stick to your main yarn)
Spare needles or waste yarn for holding stitches
One chunky-toothed zip in your preferred shade of green, blue, or grey (for hoody sizes 32-40in, zip should measure 56cm/22in; for hoody sizes 44-50in, zip should measure 61cm/24in)
Tapestry needle for weaving in ends

TENSION
Work a tension swatch as follows:
Cast on 40 sts.
In stocking st, work 48 rows of stripe pattern (see below). Bind off. Block your swatch and count the sts and rows to 10cm/4in.

28 sts and 36 rows to 10cm/4in over stocking st using 3mm needles

You must match the correct tension, or your hoody will not fit. If you have too many sts to 10cm/4in, then you need to use a larger needle. If you have too few sts to 10cm/4in, then you need to use a smaller needle. In either case you will need to prepare a new tension swatch as described above.

STRIPE PATTERN WHEN WORKING BACK AND FORTH (ALSO SHOWN ON CHART)
Rows 1-6: Using MC, work in stocking st.
Row 7: Using CC1, knit.
Row 8: Use CC2, purl.
Rows 9-14: Using MC, work in stocking st.
Row 15: Using CC3, knit.
Row 16: Using CC4, purl.
Repeat these 16 rows.

STRIPE PATTERN WHEN WORKING IN THE ROUND
As above, but all rounds are knitted. If working from chart, all rounds are read as RS.

ABBREVIATIONS
See full list of abbreviations on page 87.

PATTERN NOTES
When working the stripe pattern, it is best to break the contrast yarns after each stripe, and weave the ends in. This avoids any tightness where yarns are carried over many rounds. The MC may be carried behind the two rows of contrast stripes each time.

The pattern instructions describe how to work a crochet provisional cast on using waste yarn. You may of course use an alternative provisional cast-on method if you prefer. See **Special Techniques** (page 84) for more information and tutorials.

INSTRUCTIONS

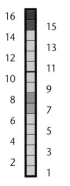

CAST ON, WORK TURNED HEM

With waste yarn and 3.25mm crochet hook, make a chain 242 (**258**, 270, **290**, 306, **318**, 330, **346**, 362, **374**) sts long. Using CC2 and 3mm needles, leaving 5 chain at each end, pick up and knit 232 (**248**, 260, **280**, 296, **308**, 320, **336**, 352, **364**) sts into the bumps on the rear of the chain.

Starting with a knit row, work back and forth in stocking st for 12 rows. Change to MC and p two rows. Starting with row 1, work in stripe pattern for 12 rows.
Use a spare 3mm needle to pick up 232 (**248**, 260, **280**, 296, **308**, 320, **336**, 352, **364**) sts in the first row of CC2 (just above the waste yarn crochet edge). Carefully unzip the crochet edge, making sure that all CC2 sts are safely on the needles.
Fold hem up along p row, placing CC2 sts behind and parallel to working sts.
Next row (RS): With MC (stripe row 13), *k together one st from front needle together with one st from back needle* repeat from * to * across the row, to create turned hem.

CHART

16	15
14	13
12	11
10	9
8	7
6	5
4	3
2	1

KEY

MC (203); Knit on RS, Purl on WS
CC1 (141); Knit on RS, Purl on WS
CC2 (FC37); Knit on RS, Purl on WS
CC3 (65); Knit on RS, Purl on WS
CC4 (FC41); Knit on RS, Purl on WS

NORTHMAVINE HOODY

2 DIVIDE FOR POCKETS, ADD WAIST SHAPING TO FRONTS AND BACK

Keeping stripe pattern correct throughout,
add pocket seam and waist shaping to right front
as follows:
Next row: With another 3mm needle k58 (**62**,
65, **70**, 74, **77**, 80, **84**, 88, **91**) sts of right front
and turn work.
Next row (WS): P58 (**62**, 65, **70**, 74, **77**, 80, **84**,
88, **91**) of right front, leaving back and left front
sts on main needle.
Working back and forth on right front sts only:
A: K to last 3 sts, k2tog, k1.
B: Work 5 rows.
Repeat steps A and B 5 more times. 52 (**56**, 59,
64, 68, **71**, 74, **78**, 82, **85**) sts.
Set right front sts aside.

With RS facing, rejoin yarn to sts on main needle.

Next row (RS): With another 3mm needle, k116
(**124**, 130, **140**, 148, **154**, 160, **168**, 176, **182**) sts
of back, remove marker and turn work.
Next row (WS): Purl to end, leaving left front sts
on main needle.
Working back and forth on back sts only:
A: K1, ssk, k to last 3 sts, k2tog, k1.
B: Work 5 rows.
Repeat steps A and B 5 more times. 104 (**112**,
118, **128**, 136, **142**, 148, **156**, 164, **170**) sts.
Set back sts aside.

With RS facing, rejoin yarn to remaining sts for
left front.
Work 2 rows in stocking st on these 58 (**62**, 65,
70, 74, **77**, 80, **84**, 88, **91**) sts.
A: K1, ssk, k to end of row.
B: Work 5 rows.
Repeat steps A and B 5 more times. 52 (**56**, 59,
64, 68, **71**, 74, **78**, 82, **85**) sts.

3 REJOIN FRONTS AND BACK, CONTINUE WAIST SHAPING

Next row (RS): Rejoin yarn to right front sts and
k across these 52 (**56**, 59, **64**, 68, **71**, 74, **78**,
82, **85**) sts, pm, k across 104 (**112**, 118, **128**,
136, **142**, 148, **156**, 164, **170**) sts of back, pm,
k across 52 (**56**, 59, **64**, 68, **71**, 74, **78**, 82, **85**)
left front sts. 208 (**224**, 236, **256**, 272, **284**, 296,
312, 328, **340**) sts.
Next row (WS): P to end.

A: *K to 3 sts before marker, k2tog, k1, slm, k1,
ssk* repeat from * to * once more, k to end.
B: Work 7 rows.
Repeat steps A and B twice more. 196 (**212**, 224,
244, 260, **272**, 284, **300**, 316, **328**) sts.
Work in pattern for 5cm/2in, ending with a WS
row. (Consult schematic: if you would like to add
length to garment body, do so here).

4 WORK BUST INCREASES, COMPLETE BODY

A: *K to 1 st before marker, m1, k1, slm, k1, m1*
repeat from * to * once more, knit to end.
B: Work 6 rows.
Repeat steps A and B 6 (**6**, 6, **5**, 5, **6**, 6, **6**, 6, **6**)
more times. 224 (**240**, 252, **268**, 284, **300**, 312,
328, 344, **356**) sts.

All sizes
Work as set until garment measures 43 (**43**, 43,
44, 44, **46**, 46, **46**, 46, 46) cm/17 (**17**, 17, **17.5**,
17.5, **18**, 18, **18**, 18, 18) in, ending with a stripe
row 8 or 16.

5 SET ASIDE STS AT BODY UNDERARMS

Moving sts around needles without knitting, slip
7 (**7**, 7, **7**, 8, **8**, 8, **9**, 10, **10**) sts each side of the
two side markers to waste yarn. Two sets of 14
(**14**, 14, **14**, 16, **16**, 16, **18**, 20, **20**) underarm sts
on waste yarn, 49 (**53**, 56, **60**, 63, **67**, 70, **73**,
76, **79**) sts for each front and 98 (**106**, 112, **120**,
126, **134**, 140, **146**, 152, **158**) sts for back. 196
(**212**, 224, **240**, 252, **268**, 280, **292**, 304, **316**)
body sts in total.
Set body sts aside.

6 CAST ON SLEEVE, TURN HEM

With waste yarn and 3.25mm crochet hook,
make a chain 62 (**66**, 70, **74**, 78, **78**, 80, **82**,
86, **88**) sts long. Using CC2 and 3mm needles,
leaving 5 chain at each end, pick up and knit 52
(**56**, 60, **64**, 68, **68**, 70, **72**, 76, **78**) sts in the
bumps on the rear of the chain.

Now k 12 rounds.
Join in MC and k 1 round, then p 1 round.
Starting with row 1, begin working in stripe
pattern in the round for 12 rounds.

Use a spare 3mm needle to pick up 52 (**56**, 60,
64, 68, **68**, 70, **72**, 76, **78**) sts in the first row of

CC2 (just above the waste yarn crochet edge). Carefully unzip the crochet edge, making sure that all CC2 sts are safely on the needles.

Fold hem up along p row, placing CC2 sts behind and parallel to working sts.
Next round: With MC (stripe row 13), *k together one st from front together with one st from back needle* repeat from * to * across the round, to create turned hem.
Work 1 round.

7

WORK SLEEVE

A: K1, m1, k to last st, m1, k1.
B: K 5 (**5**, 5, **5**, 5, **5**, 4, **4**, 4, **4**) rounds.
Repeat steps A and B 19 (**19**, 19, **19**, 19, **21**, 22, **23**, 23, **24**) more times. 92 (**96**, 100, **104**, 108, **112**, 116, **120**, 124, **128**) sts.
Keeping stripe pattern correct as set, k until sleeve measures 43 (**43**, 43, **44**, 44, **46**, 46, **46**, 47, **48**) cm/17 (**17**, 17, **17.5**, 17.5, **18**, 18, **18**, 18.5, **19**) in (or desired sleeve length), ending with a stripe round 8 or 16, so that it matches the body. Moving sts around needles without knitting, slip 7 (**7**, 7, **7**, 8, **8**, 8, **9**, 10, **10**) sts each side of marker to waste yarn. 14 (**14**, 14, **14**, 16, **16**, 16, **18**, 20, **20**) underarm sts set aside and 78 (**82**, 86, **90**, 92, **96**, 100, **102**, 104, **108**) sts remain. Set aside. Make another sleeve in the same way.

8

JOIN BODY AND SLEEVES, PLACE RAGLAN MARKERS

Keeping stripe pattern correct throughout as set, beg with stripe row 1 or 9, join body and sleeves as foll:
Row 1 (RS): K49 (**53**, 56, **60**, 63, **67**, 70, **73**, 76, **79**) sts of right front, pm, k78 (**82**, 86, **90**, 92, **96**, 100, **102**, 104, **108**) sts of right sleeve, pm, k98 (**106**, 112, **120**, 126, **134**, 140, **146**, 152, **158**) sts of back, pm, k78 (**82**, 86, **90**, 92, **96**, 100, **102**, 104, **108**) sts of left sleeve, pm, k49 (**53**, 56, **60**, 63, **67**, 70, **73**, 76, **79**) sts of left front. 352 (**376**, 396, 420, 436, **460**, 480, **496**, 512, **532**) sts.
Row 2 (WS): P to end.

9

ADJUST ST COUNT, WORK RAGLAN SHAPING

Third and sixth sizes only
Row 3: [Knit to marker, slm] twice, k1, ssk, knit to 3 sts before marker, k2tog, k1, slm, knit to end. - (-, 394, -, -, **458**, -, -, -, -) sts.
Row 4: P to end.

Seventh, eighth, and tenth sizes only
Row 3: *Knit to 3 sts before marker, k2tog, k1, slm, knit to marker, slm, k1, ssk* repeat from * to * once more, knit to end.- (-, -, -, -, -, 476, **492**, -, **528**) sts.
Row 4: P to end.

All sizes
Work 0 (**2**, 0, **2**, 2, **0**, 0, **0**, 2, **2**) rows in pattern.
Work raglan decreases as follows:
A: *K to 3 sts before marker, ssk, k1, slm, k1, k2tog* repeat from * to* 3 more times, knit to end.
B: Purl 1 row.
Repeat steps A and B 25 (**25**, 25, **27**, 29, **31**, 33, **35**, 37, **39**) more times. 144 (**168**, 186, **196**, 196, **202**, 204, **204**, 208, **208**) sts.

10

SHAPE FRONT OPENING, COMPLETE RAGLAN SHAPING, SET UP HOOD

First size only
A (neck and raglan shaping): K1, ssk, *knit to 3 sts before marker, ssk, k1, slm, k1, k2tog* repeat from * to * 3 more times, knit to last 3 sts, k2tog, k1. Purl 1 row.
B (neck shaping only): K1, ssk, k to last 3 sts, k2tog, k1. Purl 1 row.

Repeat steps A and B 2 more times (12 rows worked in total). 108 sts.
Next row (raglan shaping only): *K to 3 sts before marker, ssk, k1, slm, k1, k2tog* repeat from * to* 3 times, knit to end. 100 sts.
Work 3 rows in stocking st.

Second to tenth sizes only
A (neck and raglan shaping): K1, ssk, *knit to 3 sts before marker, ssk, k1, slm, k1, k2tog* repeat from * to * 3 times, knit to last 3 sts, k2tog, k1.
B: Purl 1 row.
Repeat steps A and B - (**5**, 6, **6**, 6, **6**, 7, **7**, 7, **7**) more times. - (**108**, 116, **126**, 126, **132**, 124, **124**, 128, **128**) sts.
C (raglan shaping only): *K to 3 sts before marker, ssk, k1, slm, k1, k2tog* repeat from * to* 3 times, knit to end.
D: Purl 1 row.
Repeat steps C and D - (**0**, 1, **2**, 2, **2**, 1, **1**, 1, **1**) more times. - (**100**, 100, **102**, 102, **108**, 108, **108**, 112, **112**) sts.

All sizes
Next row: K to end, removing raglan markers.
Next row (WS): P50 (**50**, 50, **51**, 51, **54**, 54, **54**, 56, **56**), pm (centre hood), p50 (**50**, 50, **51**, 51, **54**, 54, **54**, 56, **56**).

11 SHAPE AND COMPLETE HOOD

A: Knit to 1 st before hood marker, m1, k1, slm, k1, m1, k to end.
B: Work 3 rows in stocking st .
Repeat steps A and B 9 more times.
120 (**120**, 120, **122**, 122, **128**, 128, **128**, 132, **132**) sts.
Work straight until hood measures 27 (**27**, 27, **28**, 28, **28**, 28, **29**, 29, **29**) cm/10.5 (**10.5**, 10.5, **11**, 11, **11**, 11, **11.5**, 11.5, **11.5**) in, ending with a WS row.
Divide sts onto two needles with 60 (**60**, 60, **61**, 61, **64**, 64, **64**, 66, **66**) sts on each needle. Working from the RS, graft together these two sets of sts using Kitchener stitch, thus joining the hood.

12 WORK POCKETS

From the RS, with lining yarn and 3mm needle, starting at the bottom of the side seam opening, puk 42 sts around right pocket edge opening, pm for start of round, and join for working in the round.
Knit 45 rounds.
Round 46: K21, pm, k to end of round.
A: K1, k2tog, k to 3 sts before marker, ssk, k1, slm, k1, k2tog, k to last 3 sts, ssk, k1. 38 sts.
B: Knit 1 round.
Repeat steps A and B 2 more times. 30 sts.
Place first 15 sts of round on one needle, and last 15 sts on a second needle and with WS of pocket facing each other and RS facing you, graft sts together using Kitchener stitch. Turn pocket to the inside.
Work left pocket in exactly the same way.

13 WORK FRONT EDGE AND HOOD FACINGS

*Please read notes in **Special Techniques** (page 84) about how to work puk before starting this section.*
With CC4, 3mm circular needle (100-150cm/40-60in long), with the RS of the work facing, and beg at bottom right front edge, puk 3 sts for every 4 rows up right front, along right front edge opening, up right side of hood, down left side of hood, down left front edge opening, and down left side of front to bottom left edge.
Beg with a p row, work in stocking st for 6 rows, ending with a k row. Keep these sts live on needle: do not break yarn.

Now, turn the work to the WS. You will see the CC4 back-loops of the sts you picked up for the right side of your facing. With a second 3mm circular needle (100-150cm/40-60in long), pu each of these loops without knitting and place them on your needle. With CC3, and beg with a k row, work in stocking st for 5 rows, ending with a k row. Break yarn.

Turn work to the RS. You have 2 sets of facing sts, sitting parallel to one another.
Next row (RS): With CC4, *k 1 st from front needle together with 1 st from back needle* repeat from * to * across the row to close facing. Break yarn, keeping the remaining sts live on needle.

14 WORK I-CORD EDGING ALONG BOTTOM EDGE AND FACINGS

With CC4 and 3mm needle, working from the RS, and beg at corner of bottom right front edge, puk 4 sts along bottom of right front facing, puk 232 (**248**, 260, **280**, 296, **308**, 320, **336**, 352, **364**) sts in turned purl sts around bottom edge of hem, puk 4 sts along bottom left front facing. Break yarn. Without knitting, move sts along bottom edge of garment around needles so that you can begin row in spot beneath right pocket.

Rejoin CC4 and, with 3.25mm dpn, working from the RS, work i-cord bind off (see **Special Techniques**, page 84) across sts of right bottom edge. When you reach corner between right bottom edge and right front edge, work plain i-cord for 1 row in order to ease i-cord round the corner. Work i-cord bind off along sts up right front edge of garment, along right front edge opening, and up right front edge of hood. Now work i-cord bind off down left front edge of hood, along left front edge opening, and down left front edge of garment. When you reach the corner between left front edge and left bottom edge, work plain i-cord for 1 row in order to ease i-cord round the corner. Work i-cord bind off along remaining sts of bottom edge. When no garment sts remain, (3 i-cord sts only), work a plain i-cord for 2 rows, fasten off and join neatly to start of round.

15 FINISH CUFFS

Return to right sleeve. With CC4 and 3.25mm needle, puk 52 (**56**, 60, **64**, 68, **68**, 70, **72**, 76, **78**) in turned purl sts around bottom edge of cuff. Work i-cord bind off across all sts. Do the same for the left sleeve cuff.

16 FINISHING

Graft sts at underarms together using Kitchener stitch. Weave in all ends to the back of the work. Soak garment in tepid water with wool wash to allow the sts to relax and bloom. Rinse carefully in cold water. Press between towels to remove water. Shape garment to correct dimensions, and pin out flat, or dry over dress form. Leave to dry completely. Pin out, then stitch zip into place along inside front edge facings.

Enjoy your Northmavine Hoody!

NORTHMAVINE HAP

A warm hap, with dramatic waves of colour inspired by the bright greens and blues of the rocks and water which shape the rugged landscape of Northmavine.

SIZE
One size only
Wingspan: 160cm/63in
Length from nape to tip: 61cm/24in
The size of the hap can be adjusted easily, if required, by adding or removing repeats of the 24-row pattern. Don't forget that you will need to adjust your yarn quantities to reflect any changes.

MATERIALS
Jamieson & Smith 2 Ply Jumper Weight (100% Shetland Wool; 118m/25g balls)

MC: SHADE 203
    3 x 25g balls
CC1: SHADE 141
    1 x 25g ball
CC2: SHADE FC37
    1 x 25g ball
CC3: SHADE 65
    1 x 25g ball
CC4: SHADE FC41
    1 x 25g ball

4mm circular needles (UK 8/US 6) in the following length:
1 x 100cm/40in long
2 pairs of stitch markers of different types/colours (A and B)
4 stitch markers of another type/colour (C)
Waste yarn (a smooth cotton 4 ply will work best as it won't stick to your main yarn)
Tapestry needle for weaving in ends

TENSION
Work a tension swatch as follows:
Using MC, cast on 2 sts.
Work from pattern instructions below, until row 12 of the main pattern has been worked for the second time. Break MC and slip all sts to a long length of smooth waste yarn. Tie the ends of the waste yarn together so that your stitches are secure, but you can stretch the mini-shawl out firmly. Block your swatch firmly, allow to dry fully and unpin. Count the stitches and rows to 10cm/4in.

20 sts and 30 rows to 10cm/4in over pattern using 4mm needles

Tension is not crucial for the fit of this project, but will affect yarn quantities used.
Making a swatch will allow you to familiarise yourself with the rhythm of the pattern and its colour changes. If your tension is correct, simply return your stitches to 4mm needles and continue with row 13 of the pattern as set.

PATTERN NOTES
This pattern includes several shade changes, which will result in many ends to weave in. To do this as neatly as possible, I recommend knitting together the old and new shades on the first st of the row; then break off the old shade (leaving a length of yarn of at least 9cm/3.5in) and continue in pattern with the new shade. Doing this helps to maintain a neat, flexible and consistent-looking edge at the place where shades are joined, and will help when weaving in ends.

ABBREVIATIONS
See full list of abbreviations on page 87.

INSTRUCTIONS

1

GARTER TAB CAST ON

With MC, cast on 2 sts. Work in garter stitch for 6 rows. Turn work 90 degrees and puk 3 sts from row-end edge of garter ridges, turn again and puk 2 sts from cast-on edge. 7 sts.

2

PLACE A AND B MARKERS, INCREASE STS

Row 1 (RS): With MC, k1, pmA, k2, pmB, k1, pmB, k2, pmA, k1 ('A' markers set row ends; 'B' markers indicate centre st).

Row 2 (WS): K1, slmA, kfb, k to last st before next marker A, kfb, slmA, k1. 9 sts.

Row 3: K1, slmA, yo, k3, yo, slmB, k1, slmB, yo, k3, yo, slmA, k1. 13 sts.

Row 4: K1, slmA, kfb, k to last st before next marker A, kfb, slmA, k1. 15 sts.

Row 5: K1, slmA, yo, k6, yo, slmB, k1, slmB, yo, k6, yo, slmA, k1. 19 sts.

Row 6: K1, slmA, kfb, p to last st before next marker A, kfb, slmA, k1. 21 sts.

Row 7: K1, slmA, yo, k9, yo, slmB, k1, slmB, yo, k9, yo, slmA, k1. 25 sts.

Row 8: K1, slmA, kfb, p to last st before next marker A, kfb, slmA, k1. 27 sts.

3

SET CHART POSITIONS, PLACE C MARKERS, BEGIN WORKING FROM CHART

The following lace pattern is also shown on the chart.

Row 1 (RS): Using CC1, k1, slmA, yo, pmC, k to marker B (don't slip it yet), pmC, yo, slmB, k1, slmB, yo, pmC, k to marker A (don't slip it yet), pmC, yo, slmA, k1. 31 sts.

Row 2 (WS): Using CC1, k1, slmA, kfb, slmC, k to marker C, slmC, k1, slmB, k1, slmB, k1, slmC, k to marker C, slmC, kfb, slmA, k1. 33 sts.

Row 3: Change to CC2, k1, slmA, yo, k to marker C, slmC, *[k2tog] twice, [yo, k1] 4 times, [k2tog] twice*, slmC, yo, k to marker B, slmB, k1, slmB, k to marker C, yo, slmC, *[k2tog] twice, [yo, k1] 4 times, [k2tog] twice*, slmC, k to marker A, yo, slmA, k1. 37 sts.

Row 4: Using CC2, p1, slmA, kfb, p to marker C, slmC, p to marker C, slmC, p to marker B, slmB, p1, slmB, p to marker C, slmC, p to marker C, slmC, p to last st before marker A, kfb, slmA, p1. 39 sts.

Row 5: Change to MC, k1, slmA, yo, k to marker C, slmC, k to marker C, slmC, yo, k to marker B, slmB, k1, slmB, k to marker C, yo, slmC, k to marker C, slmC, k to marker A, yo, slmA, k1. 43 sts.
Row 6: Using MC, as row 4. 45 sts.
Row 7: Change to CC3, as row 5. 49 sts.
Row 8: Using CC3, k1, slmA, kfb, k to marker C, slmC, k to marker C, slmC, k to marker B, slmB, k1, slmB, k to marker C, slmC, k to marker C, slmC, k to last st before marker A, kfb, slmA, k1. 51 sts.
Row 9: Change to CC4, as row 3. 55 sts.
Row 10: Using CC4, as row 4. 57 sts.
Row 11: Change to MC, as row 5. 61 sts.
Row 12: Using MC, as row 4. 63 sts.
Row 13: Change to CC1, as row 5. 67 sts.
Row 14: Using CC1, as row 8. 69 sts.
Row 15: Change to CC2, k1, slmA, yo, k to 12 sts before marker C, *[k2tog] twice, [yo, k1] 4 times, [k2tog] twice*, slmC, rep from * to * to marker C, slmC, yo, k to marker B, slmB, k1, slmB, k to marker C, yo, slmC, rep from * to * to marker C, slmC, rep from * to * once more, k to marker A, yo, slmA, k1. 73 sts.

Row 16: Using CC2, as row 4. 75 sts.
Row 17: Change to MC, as row 5. 79 sts.
Row 18: Using MC, as row 4. 81 sts.
Row 19: Change to CC3, as row 5. 85 sts.
Row 20: Using CC3, as row 8. 87 sts.
Row 21: Change to CC4, as row 15. 91 sts.
Row 22: Using CC4, as row 4. 93 sts.
Row 23: Change to MC, as row 5. 97 sts.
Row 24: Using MC, as row 4, but removing 4 marker Cs as you work. 99 sts.
Last 24 rows establish pattern (also shown on chart). Work 4 more repeats of the 24-row pattern, as described below, then work rows 1-12 once more. 423 sts.

Each 24-row repeat increases the total stitch count by 72 sts. This means that for each 24-row repeat the pattern (given between * and * on rows 3 and 15) between marker Cs is repeated 3 more times on each side.
In the second 24-row repeat, there will be 48 sts between marker Cs, and the pattern will be repeated 4 times on each side of the shawl.
Total sts at end of second repeat: 171 sts.

CHART (CONT)

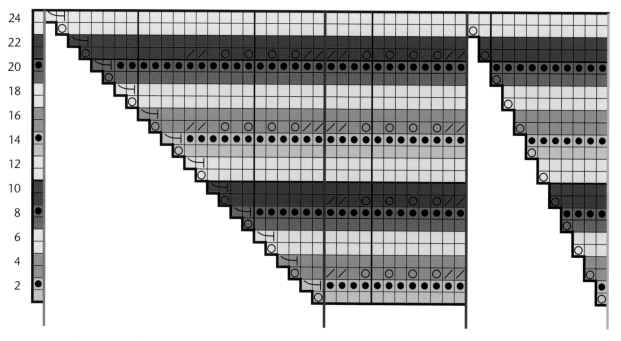

A marker - edge st   C markers around repeats   B marker

On the third 24-row repeat, there will be 84 sts between marker Cs, and the pattern will be worked 7 times on each side of the shawl. Total sts at end of third repeat: 243 sts.

On the fourth 24-row repeat, there will be 120 sts between marker Cs, and the pattern will be repeated 10 times on each side of the shawl. Total sts at end of fourth repeat: 315 sts.

On the fifth 24-row repeat there will be 156 sts between marker Cs, and the pattern will be repeated 13 times on each side of the shawl. Total sts at end of fifth repeat: 387 sts.

At the start of the final half-repeat there will be 192 sts between marker Cs, and the pattern will be repeated 16 times on each side of the shawl. Total sts at end of half-repeat: 423 sts.

4 COMPLETE HAP

With MC, work in garter stitch for 4 rows (k every row).
Bind-off all sts using the sewn bind-off method (see **Special Techniques**, page 84).

5 BLOCKING AND FINISHING

Weave in all ends, but do not trim. Soak hap in tepid water and wool wash for at least 20 minutes. Press between towels to remove water. Stretch and block vigorously using pins and blocking wires, stretching out the openwork stitches. Allow to dry fully, then unpin and trim ends.

Enjoy your Northmavine Hap!

KEY

☐ MC (203); Knit on RS, purl on WS

☐ CC1 (141); Knit on RS, purl on WS

☐ CC2 (FC37); Knit on RS, purl on WS

▨ CC3 (65); Knit on RS, purl on WS

■ CC4 (FC41); Knit on RS, purl on WS

⊙ Using shade as indicated, purl on RS, knit on WS

╱ Using shade as indicated, k2tog

⊢ Kfb

◯ Yarnover

CHART

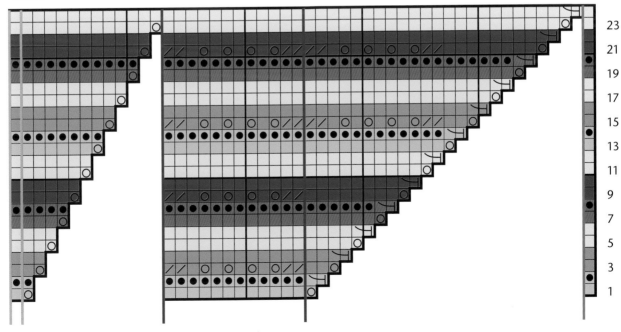

B markers around centre st   C markers around repeats   A marker - edge st

*The excavations at Old Scatness slowly uncovered a
site of world-class archaeological significance that
had been in continuous human habitation for more
than four thousand years.*

Discovering Scatness

Old Scatness has been a place of shelter for the people of Shetland from the Bronze Age, through Iron Age, Pictish and Viking eras.

One day in 1975, workmen were extending an access road for the newly-developing airport at Sumburgh, when they began to dig through an earthy mound. As their machines cut short and hit stone, it became immediately apparent that what they were digging through was not a natural mound at all, but was, in all likelihood, archaeology. Tom Henderson (then curator of the Shetland Museum) was consulted and cannily recognised the stones as being those of an Iron Age broch. The airport road was realigned, the site was earmarked as being of archeological importance and subsequently lay untouched for twenty years.

In 1995, through the efforts of the Shetland Amenity Trust, funding finally became available to enable the ground-breaking excavation of the site. At that point, it was assumed that what would be found would be, as Tom Henderson had predicted, a broch, but what was discovered exceeded everyone's expectations. Over the next decade, the excavations at Old Scatness slowly uncovered a site of world-class archaeological significance that had been in continuous human habitation for over four thousand years.

A PLACE OF SHELTER

Bronze Age humans had once farmed the site, finding the light, sandy soils of Shetland's South Mainland ideal for raising crops. Then, some two thousand years later, Iron Age inhabitants had constructed a large broch (an intriguingly complex, multi-storey stone structure of which over eighty are known to exist in Shetland). A village of aisled roundhouses grew up around the broch, and later Pictish dwellers adapted both broch and village to their own purposes, re-using the stone for their own buildings, developing walls and passageways, and re-forming the circular constructions into their own characteristic wheel-shaped dwellings.

Old Scatness was then inhabited by Vikings and, while traces of a traditionally-shaped longhouse were discovered on site, there was also evidence that the Norse settlers had adapted the round Pictish buildings to their own purposes, using them as spaces for the production of woven cloth and other textiles (a particularly important discovery in one of the wheelhouses was a series of bored-soapstone weights arranged just as they would have been, to hold the warp threads of a Viking loom).

RE-BUILDING, RE-WORKING, RE-MAKING

What was discovered through the Old Scatness excavations was of major importance. Cutting-edge dating techniques suggested that Shetland's brochs must have been constructed between 400-200BC – much earlier than previously assumed, prompting crucial reinterpretation of other sites. But work did not end with excavation. Through a series of impressive collaborative projects, Shetland Amenity Trust enabled locals and visitors alike to play an integral role in Old Scatness, making its archaeology and cultural heritage uniquely accessible and engaging.

Using the original materials of the site, and working closely with archaeologists and historians, experienced stone workers first carefully reconstructed some of the site's Pictish dwellings. Research then began to be conducted into the kinds of domestic textiles and other objects that were once produced at Old Scatness, and ancient crafts of soapstone working, pottery, weaving, cord making, and sprang (an intriguing ancient combination of knitting and weaving) were investigated and later practiced by exceptionally skilled on-site guides.

Like the learning processes involved in all crafts, these acts of re-building, re-working, and re-making brought important new insights into the purposes and uses of the domestic spaces of the site, as well as into the everyday lives of the humans that once inhabited it. Visiting Old Scatness today, you not only find world-class archaeology made publicly accessible, but you can sit by a blazing peat fire in a surprisingly cosy Pictish wheelhouse; try your hand at Viking tablet weaving with one of the site's talented craftspeople; listen to the whirl of the wind and waves outside, and imagine how ordinary life might have looked in Shetland several thousand years ago. It is a remarkable place.

COLOUR AND CONSTRUCTION

My starting points when beginning to think about producing designs inspired by the ancient spaces of Scatness were its multiple layers of history and archaeology, the cyclical rhythms of its continuously inhabited landscape, and the circles-within-circles that define its vernacular architecture. After a tour around the site with brilliant local archaeologist, Chris Dyer, I couldn't stop thinking about an aerial photograph he had showed me of Old Scatness under excavation. To me, this photograph called to mind a series of tam crowns, with their characteristic concentric circles and wedge-shaped segments (my immediate thought was of the images of tams in Sheila McGregor's *Traditional Fair Isle Knitting*).

Most of the site's numerous circular buildings can be seen on the aerial photograph, but one in particular stood out. Inside the Iron Age broch, later Pictish dwellers had constructed an attractive clover-shaped structure, which just like a tam crown, was composed of seven 'leaves'. I based the surface design of my Scatness Tam crown on the lines and curves of the ancient wheelhouse, with spokes and cells arranged around a central 'hearth'.

KNITTING BACK IN TIME

The motif around the body of the tam is inspired by the four-leaf-clover design of a mould recovered from the Viking and Norse phases of the Old Scatness site (SF7714). Casts from this mould would have produced positive impressions to be used, singly or in sequence, as decorative mounts on leather. I liked that the petal and leaf shapes of the crown were to be echoed

DISCOVERING SCATNESS

in similar motifs around the body, and if one were thinking fancifully while making the tam, one might imagine beginning with the design-motifs of the Vikings, and then knitting back in time through Pictish and Iron-Age circles.

Just like the tam, the Scatness Tunic is constructed in the round. It features the Viking mould motif around the yoke, is edged with deep circular 'walls' of corrugated ribbing and is finished off with the decorative spokes and circles of 'wheelhouse buttons', which are a lot of fun to make.

OF LIGHT AND LANDSCAPE

Colour was just as important to me as construction when producing these designs. As the year turns toward winter, Shetland puts on one of its most beautiful shows. The sun hangs low and luminous; clouds skitter rapidly across the sky, and the whole landscape shifts rapidly in and out of light and shadow. There are deep, heathery colours on the hill and an urgency in the air – the very light and landscape convey that familiar autumn feeling of having to make adequate preparation against the dark and cold. But equally, it is a time when it is wonderful to be outdoors.

While the cities of Britain are wrapped in gloomy October fog, there is really nothing better than a brisk Shetland walk on a bright golden day, or to stand alone on a stretch of sand watching the waves break against a stunning sunset streaked with burgundy and rust.

These are the colours of my two Scatness designs. The shades I selected are some of my all-time Jamieson & Smith favourites: FC12 – a mossy green blended with bright flecks of gold; FC14 – a deep blue enlivened with flashes of turquoise and fuschia; and FC58 – a brown that is not brown at all, but rather a rich composite of multiple, shimmering hues.

This rich, mercurial palette is probably what I most immediately call to mind when I think of the 'colours of Shetland'. Perhaps this is because the complexity of these shades seems best revealed against the lovely northern light; or perhaps because they are quintessentially autumnal, suggesting a time for hunkering down and knitting. I do hope you enjoy them.

AUTHOR'S NOTE

With grateful thanks to Chris Dyer and Jane Outram for an inspirational introduction to Old Scatness.

RESOURCES

Stephen J Dockrill, Julie M Bond, Val E Turner, Louise D Brown, Daniel J Bashford, Julia E Cussans, Rebecca A Nicholson, *Excavations at Old Scatness, Shetland, vol.1: The Pictish and Viking Settlement* (2010)

Val E Turner, 'Old Scatness: The Bronze Age, Picts and Vikings all in one Location' *60 North* (Summer, 2012).

Sheila McGregor, *Traditional Fair Isle Knitting* (2003 edn)

PHOTOGRAPHY

All images © Kate Davies Designs and www.shetland.org

SCATNESS
TUNIC AND TAM

The colours of the Scatness Tunic and Tam were inspired by the rich palette of the South Mainland landscape as the year turns towards winter. The dwellings of Old Scatness and decorative Viking leatherwork found on the site provided the inspiration for the colourwork motifs.

PATTERN » TUNIC PAGE 74, TAM PAGE 80

SCATNESS TUNIC

A tunic cardigan with Fair Isle yoke, corrugated rib and signature wheelhouse buttons.

SIZES

This tunic has been designed to fit with 2.5-5cm/1-2in of positive ease (to allow the wearing of light layers underneath). For the best fit, select the size above your actual bust measurement.

TO FIT BUST

76	**81**	86	**91**	97	**102**	107	**112**	117	**122**	cm
30	**32**	34	**36**	38	**40**	42	**44**	46	**48**	in

ACTUAL BUST

81	**88**	95	**99**	103	**106**	114	**117**	121	**128**	cm
32	**34.75**	37.5	**39**	40.5	**42**	44.75	**46**	47.5	**50.5**	in

LENGTH TO UNDERARM

41	**41**	41	**43**	43	**45**	45	**45**	45	**45**	cm
16	**16**	16	**17**	17	**17.75**	17.75	**17.75**	17.75	**17.75**	in

YOKE DEPTH AT BACK

17	**17**	18	**18**	19	**19**	20	**20**	21	**21**	cm
6.75	**6.75**	7.25	**7.25**	7.5	**7.5**	8	**8**	8.25	**8.25**	in

FINISHED LENGTH

61	**61**	62	**65**	66	**68**	68	**68**	69	**69**	cm
24	**24**	24.5	**25.5**	25.75	**26.5**	26.75	**26.75**	27.25	**27.25**	in

MATERIALS

Jamieson & Smith 2 ply Jumper Weight (100% Shetland Wool; 118m/25g balls)

MC: SHADE 202
7 (**7**, 8, **9**, 9, **10**, 11, **11**, 11, **12**) x 25g balls

CC1: SHADE FC58
2 (**3**, 3, **3**, 3, **4**, 4, **4**, 4, **4**) x 25g balls

CC2: SHADE FC14
1 (**1**, 2, **2**, 2, **2**, 2, **2**, 2, **2**) x 25g balls

CC3: SHADE FC56
1 (**1**, 2, **2**, 2, **2**, 2, **2**, 2, **2**) x 25g balls

CC4: SHADE FC55
1 (**1**, 2, **2**, 2, **2**, 2, **2**, 2, **2**) x 25g balls

CC5: SHADE FC38
1 (**1**, 2, **2**, 2, **2**, 2, **2**, 2, **2**) x 25g balls

CC6: SHADE FC12
1 x 25g balls in all sizes

3mm (UK 11/US 2-3) circular needles in the following lengths: 1 x 60cm/24in long; 3 x 80-100cm/30-40in long (for holding sts, working edging and finishing); 1 x 20cm/8in long (for working sleeve caps)
3.25mm dpn for working i-cord bind off
3.25mm (UK 10/US D/3) crochet hook
Waste yarn (a smooth cotton 4 ply will work best as it won't stick to your main yarn)
Six transparent button snaps (1-2cm/0.5in)
1.5m/1.5yd grosgrain ribbon or linen tape (3-4cm/1-1.5in) wide for button band lining
Cotton sewing thread in similar shade to ribbon.
Five (or six) plain buttons (2.5cm/1in)
Cardboard and spare lengths of yarn in your preferred shades for making covered wheelhouse buttons
Tapestry needle for weaving in ends

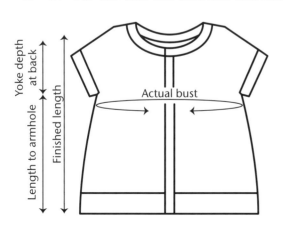

TENSION

Work 2 tension swatches as follows:

Fair Isle pattern

Cast on 54 sts and join for working in the round. Work 5 rounds in MC. Work 31 rounds from chart E, doing the marked section only once. Work 5 rounds in MC, bind off. Reinforce and cut steek, following the instructions in the **Special Techniques** section on page 84.
Block your swatch and count the sts and rounds to 10cm/4in.

28 sts and 34 rounds to 10cm/4in over Fair Isle pattern using 3mm needles

Stocking stitch

Cast on 40 sts with MC, pm and join for working in the round.
Round 1: K to end.
Repeat last round 39 more times.
Bind off. Block your swatch and count the number of sts and rounds to 10cm/4in.

28 sts and 34 rounds to 10cm/4in over stocking st using 3mm needles

You must match the correct tension in both stitch patterns, or your tunic will not fit. If you have too many sts to 10cm/4in, then you need to use a larger needle. If you have too few sts to 10cm/4in, then you need to use a smaller needle. In either case you will need to prepare a new tension swatch as described above. Getting the correct tension in one stitch pattern does not guarantee matching tension in a different stitch pattern, and you may need to use different sized needles for the two stitch patterns.

PATTERN NOTES

The pattern instructions describe how to work a crochet provisional cast on using waste yarn. You can of course use an alternative provisional cast-on method if you prefer. See **Special Techniques**, page 84, for more information.

ABBREVIATIONS

See full list of abbreviations on page 87.

INSTRUCTIONS

1

CAST ON, SET UP STEEK, WORK CORRUGATED RIB

With waste yarn and 3.25mm crochet hook, make a chain 260 (**280**, 300, **310**, 320, **330**, 350, **360**, 370, **390**) sts long. Using MC, and 3mm needles, leaving 5 chain at each end, pick up and knit 250 (**270**, 290, **300**, 310, **320**, 340, **350**, 360, **380**) sts in the bumps on the rear of the chain. Pm, and join for working in the round.

Join in CC1. Reading from right to left, work first 7 sts of row 1 of chart A (**A**, A, **A**, A, **B**, B, **B**, B, **B**), pm (these 7 sts set position of steek), work from row 1 of chart A (**A**, A, **A**, A, **B**, B, **B**, B, **B**) repeating marked section to last 3 sts, then work final 3 sts of chart.
Last round sets chart pattern. Work until round 18 (**18**, 18, **18**, 18, **24**, 24, **24**, 24, **24**) of chart is complete.

2

SET UP SIDE MARKERS, WORK SIDE SHAPING, COMPLETE BODY

Change to MC.
Next round: K7 steek sts, k61 (**66**, 71, **73**, 76, **78**, 83, **86**, 88, **93**), pm, k121 (**131**, 141, **147**, 151, **157**, 167, **171**, 177, **187**), pm, k61 (**66**, 71, **73**, 76, **78**, 83, **86**, 88, **93**) to end of round (markers now set position of side shaping).

A: K7 steek sts, slm, *k to 3 sts before next marker, ssk, k1, slm, k1, k2tog* repeat from * to * once, k to end of round.
B: K 6 rounds.
Repeat steps A and B 4 more times. 230 (**250**, 270, **280**, 290, **300**, 320, **330**, 340, **360**) sts (including 7 steek sts).
Work straight until piece measures 41 (**41**, 41, **43**, 43, **45**, 45, **45**, 45, **45**) cm/16 (**16**, 16, **17**, 17, **17.75**, 17.75, **17.75**, 17.75, **17.75**) in from cast-on edge.

3

SET ASIDE STS AT UNDERARMS

Moving sts around needles without knitting, removing side markers when you encounter them (but retaining start of round and steek markers) slip 6 (**7**, 7, **7**, 7, **8**, 8, **8**, 9, **10**) sts each side of each side marker to waste yarn. Two sets of 12 (**14**, 14, **14**, 14, **16**, 16, **16**, 18, **20**) sts set aside for underarms, 50 (**54**, 59, **61**, 64, **65**, 70, **73**, 74, **78**) sts for each front and 99 (**107**, 117, **123**, 127, **131**, 141, **145**, 149, **157**) sts for back remain, plus 7 steek sts.

4 WORK SLEEVE CAPS, SET ASIDE STS AT UNDERARMS

With waste yarn and 3.25mm crochet hook, make a chain 100 (**105**, 105, **110**, 110, **115**, 115, **120**, 130, **135**) sts long. Using MC, and 3mm needles, leaving 5 chain at each end, pick up and knit 90 (**95**, 95, **100**, 100, **105**, 105, **110**, 120, **125**) sts in the bumps on the rear of the chain. Pm, and join for working in the round.

Round 1: Reading from right to left, work from row 1 of chart C (**C**, C, **C**, C, **D**, D, **D**, D, **D**), repeating 5-st motif to end.
Last round sets chart pattern. Work until round 18 (**18**, 18, **18**, 18, **24**, 24, **24**, 24, **24**) of chart is complete.

Moving sts around needles without knitting, slip 6 (**7**, 7, **7**, 7, **8**, 8, **8**, 9, **10**) sts each side of marker to waste yarn. 12 (**14**, 14, **14**, 14, **16**, 16, **16**, 18, **20**) sts set aside at underarm and 78 (**81**, 81, **86**, 86, **89**, 89, **94**, 102, **105**) sleeve sts remain.
Make another sleeve in the same way.

5 JOIN BODY AND SLEEVES INTO YOKE

Rejoin MC to start of round, and join body and sleeves into yoke as follows:
Next round: K7 steek sts, k50 (**54**, 59, **61**, 64, **65**, 70, **73**, 74, **78**) right front sts, k78 (**81**, 81, **86**, 86, **89**, 89, **94**, 102, **105**) right sleeve sts, k99 (**107**, 117, **123**, 127, **131**, 141, **145**, 149, **157**) back sts, k78 (**81**, 81, **86**, 86, **89**, 89, **94**, 102, **105**) left sleeve sts, k50 (**54**, 59, **61**, 64, **65**, 70, **73**, 74, **78**) left front sts. 362 (**384**, 404, **424**, 434, **446**, 466, **486**, 508, **530**) sts (including 7 steek sts).

With MC, k 4 (**4**, 5, **5**, 6, **6**, 6, **6**, 6, **6**) rounds.

Next round: K7 steek sts, slm, k9 (**25**, 15, **8**, 19, **17**, 13, **20**, 19, **14**), *k2tog, k3 (**3**, 4, **5**, 7, **11**, 14, **17**, 20, **24**)* repeat from * to * 66 (**64**, 60, **56**, 42, **30**, 26, **22**, 20, **18**) more times, k2tog, k to end of round. 294 (**318**, 342, **366**, 390, **414**, 438, **462**, 486, **510**) sts (including 7 steek sts).

6 WORK YOKE FROM CHART

Round 1: Reading from right to left, work across row 1 of chart E, repeating marked section 11 (**12**, 13, **14**, 15, **16**, 17, **18**, 19, **20**) times in total. Last round sets chart E pattern. Continue to work from chart E as set until chart row 31 is complete.

Change to MC and k 1 round.

7 WORK FIRST DECREASE ROUND

Next round: K7 steek sts, slm, *k2, k2tog* repeat from * to * to final 3 sts, k3. 223 (**241**, 259, **277**, 295, **313**, 331, **349**, 367, **385**) sts (including 7 steek sts).

K 4 (**4**, 5, **5**, 6, **6**, 7, **7**, 8, **8**) rounds.

8 WORK SECOND DECREASE ROUND

First, and third to tenth sizes only
Next round: K7 steek sts, slm, *k2 (-, 1, **1**, 1, **1**, 1, **1**, 1, **1**), k2tog* repeat from * to * to end of round. 169 (-, 175, **187**, 199, **211**, 223, **235**, 247, **259**) sts (including 7 steek sts).

Second size only
Next round: K7 steek sts, slm, k6, *k2tog, k1* repeat from * to * 73 more times, k to end. 167 sts (including 7 steek sts).

All sizes
K 4 (**4**, 5, **5**, 6, **6**, 7, **7**, 8, **8**) rounds.

9 WORK THIRD DECREASE ROUND

First size only
Next round: K7 steek sts, slm, k2tog, k to last 2 sts, k2tog. 167 sts (including 7 steek sts).

Second size only
K 1 round.

Third to fifth, ninth and tenth sizes only
Next round: K7 steek sts, slm, *k2tog, k- (-, 19, **7**, 4, -, -, -, 1, **1**)* repeat from * to * to end. - (-, 167, **167**, 167, -, -, -, 167, **175**) sts (including 7 steek sts).

Sixth and eighth sizes only

Next round: K7 steek sts, slm, k- (-, -, -, -, **15**, -, **12**, -, -), *k2tog, k- (-, -, -, -, **2**, -, **1**, -, -)* repeat from * to * - (-, -, -, -, **43**, -, **67**, -, -) more times, k to end. 167 sts (including 7 steek sts).

Seventh size only

Next round: K7 steek sts, slm, k6, [k2tog, k1] 10 times, [k2tog, k2] 36 times, [k2tog, k1] 10 times, k to end. 167 sts (including 7 steek sts).

All sizes

K 1 (**1**, 1, **1**, 2, **2**, 2, **2**, 3, **3**) rounds.

Tenth size only

Next round: K7 steek sts, slm, k20, *k2tog, k16* repeat from * to * 7 more times, k to end. 167 sts (including 7 steek sts).

All sizes

You should now have 167sts (including 7 steek sts).

10 WORK SHORT ROWS.

Before beginning next step, familiarise yourself with the instructions for short rows in the **Special Techniques** section, on page 84.

Short row 1 (RS): K7 steek sts, slm, k120, turn, leaving remaining sts unworked.
Short row 2 (WS): P80, turn.
Short row 3: K77, turn.
Short row 4: P74, turn.
Short row 5: K71, turn.
Short row 6: P68, turn.

Next round (partial): K to end of round marker, closing gaps of all short rows.
Next round: K a complete round, closing gaps of all short rows.

11 FINAL DECREASE ROUND

Next round: K7 steek sts, slm, *k6, k2tog* repeat from * to * to end. 147 sts (including 7 steek sts).

12 BIND OFF NECK STS

Next round: With MC, bind off 7 steek sts, then bind off 140 neck sts.
(All sts are bound off to give neckline strength and structure.)

13 CUT STEEKS

Return to provisionally cast-on sts at tunic bottom edge and, using a 3mm needle, pick up 250 (**270**, 290, **300**, 310, **320**, 340, **350**, 360, **380**) sts in the first row of MC (just above the waste yarn crochet edge). Carefully unzip the crochet edge making sure that all MC sts are safely on the needle. Join in MC to start of round and bind off first 7 sts of round (steek sts). Keep remaining sts live on needle.

Following instructions to reinforce and cut steeks from **Special Techniques** section on page 84, cut the steeks for front opening. With your iron on the wool setting, give the garment a light steam on the reverse to allow the sts to relax.

14 WORK BUTTON BANDS

With RS facing, using MC and picking up sts in the gap between end of steek and beginning of pattern (see **Special Techniques**, page 84), starting at cast on edge and working up toward neck edge puk 133 (**133**, 138, **143**, 148, **148**, 153, **153**, 158, **158**) sts along right front edge opening.
Row 1 (WS): Reading from left to right, work from row 1 of chart F, repeating marked section 26 (**26**, 27, **28**, 29, **29**, 30, **30**, 31, **31**) times in total.
Row 2 (RS): Reading from right to left, work from row 2 of chart F, repeating marked section 26 (**26**, 27, **28**, 29, **29**, 30, **30**, 31, **31**) times in total.
Last 2 rows set chart F pattern. Continue to work from chart as set until row 12 is complete.
Row 13 (WS): Using CC1, p to end.
Keep these sts live on needles.

Work the left button band in the same way, starting to puk at neck edge, and ending at cast-on edge.

15 WORK NECK EDGING

With RS facing, using MC, starting at neck edge of right front button band, and picking up sts in the gap between end of steek and beginning of pattern where relevant, puk 148 sts around neck edge.

Row 1 (WS): Reading from left to right, work from row 1 of chart F, repeating marked section 29 times in total.

Row 2 (RS): Reading from right to left, work from row 2 of chart F, repeating marked section 29 times in total.

Last 2 rows set chart F pattern. Continue to work from chart as set until row 12 is complete.

Row 13 (WS): Using CC1, p to end.

Keep these sts live on needles.

16 WORK I-CORD EDGINGS

Sleeves

Using a 3mm needle, pick up 90 (**95**, 95, **100**, 100, **105**, 105, **110**, 120, **125**) sts in the first row of MC (just above the waste yarn crochet edge). Carefully unzip the crochet edge making sure that all MC sts are safely on the needle. Join in CC1 and k 1 round. With CC1 and 3.25mm dpn, bind off all sts using i-cord bind off (see **Special Techniques**, on page 84).

Body

With CC1, working from the RS, and beg at corner of bottom left front edge, puk 6 sts along bottom of left front button band, slip 243 (**263**, 283, **293**, 303, **313**, 333, **343**, 353, **373**) sts from provisional cast

on at bottom edge of hem to lh needle. Knit across these sts and puk 6 sts in bottom of right front button band. Break yarn. Without knitting, move sts along bottom edge of garment around needles to begin round at point below right underarm.

Rejoin CC1 and, with 3.25mm dpn, working from the RS, work i-cord bind off across sts of right bottom edge. When you reach corner between right bottom edge and right front edge, work plain i-cord for 1 row in order to ease i-cord round the corner. Work i-cord bind off along sts up right front edge of garment. When you reach the corner between right front edge and neck, work plain i-cord for 1 row in order to ease i-cord round the corner. Work i-cord bind off around neck. When you reach the corner between neck and left front edge, work plain i-cord for 1 row in order to ease i-cord round the corner. Now work i-cord bind off down left front edge and, when you reach the corner between left front edge and bottom edge, work plain i-cord for 1 row in order to ease i-cord round the corner. Work i-cord bind off along remaining sts of bottom edge.

When no garment sts remain (3 i-cord sts only), work a plain i-cord for 2 rows, fasten off and join neatly to start of round.

CHART E: YOKE PATTERN

17 FINISHING

Weave in ends to the back of the work. Using back stitch and MC, lightly stitch down steek edges to reverse of work, away from button bands. Soak garment in tepid water with wool wash to allow the sts to relax and bloom. Rinse carefully in cold water. Press garment between towels to remove water. Shape garment to correct dimensions and pin out flat. Leave to dry completely.

Measure your button bands carefully and cut your lining strip to these measurements, plus 1cm/0.5in (allowing space to turn the raw ends in and leave a scant 2-3mm/0.1in for stitching at top and bottom). Pin out lining strips, paying particular attention to the top and bottom of each strip, which should reach as closely as possible to the edges of the button bands. Now sew lining strips in place using invisible slip-stitch.

Mark out 5 (or 6) positions for buttons and fasteners with pins. Sew the bottom of fasteners in place along the front of the right button band. Stitch the top of fasteners in corresponding place along the underside of left button band.

Following instructions in **Wheelhouse Buttons Tutorial** on page 82, make 5 (or 6) wheelhouse buttons. Stitch wheelhouse buttons in place along the top of left button band, corresponding to placement of snap fasteners.

Enjoy your Scatness Tunic!

KEY

- MC (202); Knit on RS, Purl on WS
- CC1 (FC58); Knit on RS, Purl on WS
- CC2 (FC14); Knit on RS, Purl on WS
- CC3 (FC56); Knit on RS, Purl on WS
- CC4 (FC55); Knit on RS, Purl on WS
- CC5 (FC38); Knit on RS, Purl on WS
- CC6 (FC12); Knit on RS, Purl on WS
- ⊙ Using shade as indicated; Purl on RS, Knit on WS
- ☐ Pattern repeat

CHART F
(ROW 1 IS WS)

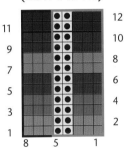

CHART D

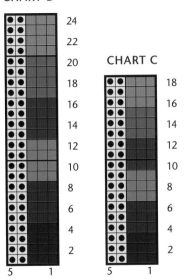

CHART C

CHART B:
STEEK AND RIBBING

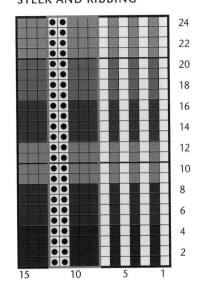

CHART A:
STEEK AND RIBBING

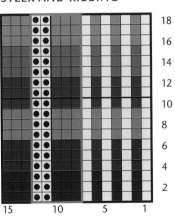

SCATNESS TAM

A richly-coloured tam, inspired by the autumnal landscape of the South Mainland and the distinctive petal-shaped walls of the dwellings at Old Scatness.

SIZE
One size only
To fit average head: 53-56cm/21-22in
Actual brim circumference: 51cm/20in

MATERIALS
Jamieson & Smith 2 Ply Jumper Weight (100% Shetland Wool; 118m/25g balls)

- **MC:** SHADE 202
  - 2 x 25g ball
- **CC1:** SHADE FC58
  - 1 x 25g ball
- **CC2:** SHADE FC14
  - 1 x 25g ball
- **CC3:** SHADE FC56
  - 1 x 25g ball
- **CC4:** SHADE FC55
  - 1 x 25g ball
- **CC5:** SHADE FC38
  - 1 x 25g ball
- **CC6:** SHADE FC12
  - 1 x 25g ball
- **CC7:** SHADE 1A
  - 1 x 25g ball

Small quantity (less than 46m/50yds) of soft 4 ply yarn for brim lining. Sample used Orkney Angora 4 ply (100% angora; 400m/50g balls) in shade Silver-grey

3mm (UK 11/US 2-3) circular needles in the following lengths: 2 x 40cm/16in long
3mm (UK 11/US 2-3) dpns (for finishing crown)
3.25mm (UK 10/US D/3) crochet hook
Waste yarn (a smooth cotton 4 ply will work best as it won't stick to your main yarn)
Stitch markers
Tapestry needle for weaving in ends

TENSION
28 sts and 34 rounds to 10cm/4in over Fair Isle pattern in the round using 3mm needles

ABBREVIATIONS
See full list of abbreviations on page 87.

PATTERN NOTES
The pattern instructions describe how to work a crochet provisional cast on using waste yarn. You may, of course, use an alternative provisional cast-on method if you prefer. See **Special Techniques**, page 84, for more information and tutorials.

INSTRUCTIONS

1

CAST ON, WORK BRIM
With waste yarn and 3.25mm crochet hook, make a chain 122 sts long. Using lining yarn and 3mm needles, leaving 5 chain at each end, pick up and knit 112 sts in the bumps on the rear of the chain. Pm and join for working in the round.
K 8 rounds.
Change to MC. K 1 round, p 1 round, k 1 round.

Next round: Join in CC2 and, reading from right to left, work row 1 from chart A, repeating motif to end of round. Last round sets chart A pattern. Continue working from chart until row 8 is complete.

Use a spare 3mm needle to pick up 112 sts in the first row of lining yarn (just above the waste yarn crochet edge). Carefully unzip the crochet edge, making sure that all the lining yarn sts are safely on the needles. Fold brim up along p round, placing cast-on sts behind and parallel to working sts.
Next row (RS): With CC1, *k together one st from front needle together with one st from back needle* repeat from * to * across the row, to create brim.

2

WORK SIDES, SHAPE CROWN
Round 1: With CC1, k1, *m1, k2* repeat from * to * to last st, m1, k1. 168 sts.
Round 2: Reading from right to left, work from row 2 of chart B, repeating marked section 6 times in total.

Last round sets chart B pattern. Continue to work from chart B until row 60 is complete, working decreases as indicated and changing to dpns when it is comfortable to do so. Stitch counts at end of decrease rounds are as follows:

Round 39: 154 sts
Round 41: 140 sts.
Round 43: 126 sts.
Round 45: 112 sts.
Round 47: 98 sts.
Round 49: 84 sts.
Round 51: 70 sts.
Round 53: 56 sts.
Round 55: 42 sts.
Round 57: 28 sts.
Round 59: 14 sts.

Next round: With CC1, [k2tog] 7 times. 7 sts. Break yarn, and draw up tightly through remaining 7 sts. Fasten off to inside of tam.

3

I-CORD BIND OFF

Weave in all ends to the back of the work. With CC1, puk 112 sts in purl round at brim edge.
Bind off all sts using the i-cord bind off method (see **Special Techniques**, page 84, for instructions on how to work i-cord bind off and puk).

4

BLOCKING

Soak tam in tepid water and wool wash to allow the sts to relax and bloom. Press between towels to remove water. You can either block tam to shape over a 25cm/10in plate or pasta bowl, or by laying flat, and pinning out the crown to a 25cm/10in diameter. Allow to fully dry.

Enjoy your Scatness Tam!

CHART A: BRIM

KEY

☐ MC (202); Knit

■ CC1 (FC58); Knit

■ CC2 (FC14); Knit

■ CC3 (FC56); Knit

■ CC4 (FC55); Knit

■ CC5 (FC38); Knit

■ CC6 (FC12); Knit

☐ CC7 (1A); Knit

⊡ Using shade as indiated; Purl

⚠ Using shade as indicated; sl2 sts knitwise, k1, p2sso

☐ Pattern repeat

CHART B: CROWN

Repeat marked section 6 times in total

TUTORIAL: WHEELHOUSE BUTTONS

These simple-to-make covered buttons echo the concentric structure of the Pictish wheelhouses at Scatness.

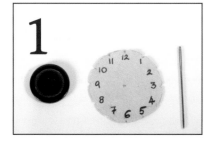

STEP 1: Select 5 (or 6) plain buttons with a 2.5cm/1in diameter.
On cardboard, draw a circle 5cm/2in in diameter (I drew around the lid of a jar). Cut out the disc; mark the centre point and with a sharp needle poke a hole through this point.
Mark numbers 1-12 around the edges of your disc, as if drawing a clock face. With a pair of sharp scissors, cut shallow notches at each of the points 1-12 (notches should be no deeper than 5mm/0.2in).

STEP 2: Cut off a 90cm/3ft length of yarn, thread your needle and draw up through the centre of the disc, leaving a short tail no longer than 1cm/0.3in.

STEP 3: Draw the yarn across the front of the disc up to notch 1.

STEP 5: Continue securing the yarn into the notches by drawing it alternately around the back circumference and across the front diameter, in the order shown in the list on the right.

WRAP NOTCHES IN THIS SEQUENCE:

6	→	7
7	→	1
1	→	2
2	→	8
8	→	9
9	→	3
3	→	4
4	→	10
10	→	11
11	→	5
5	→	6
6	→	12
12	→	11
11	→	5
5	→	4
4	→	10
10	→	9
9	→	3
3	→	2
2	→	8
8	→	7

You have now created 12 front spokes, and 12 back loops.

STEP 4: Draw the yarn around the back circumference of the disc to notch 12, secure it in the notch, then draw the yarn across the front diameter of the circle to notch 6.

STEP 6: Draw the yarn from notch 7 to the centre, securing it around the centre of the spokes.

Bring your needle up between spokes 12 and 1 as close to the centre as possible.

Then take your needle backwards over spoke 1, turn forwards and travel under spokes 1 and 12.

Now take your needle backwards over spoke 12, turn forwards and travel under spokes 12 and 11.

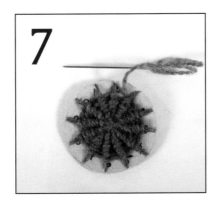

STEP 7: Continue weaving in this manner, working anti-clockwise, and drawing the yarn backward over 1 and forward under 2 spokes around the disc. This process wraps and defines the spokes, creating the ridged surface of the button covering. (If you run out of yarn, simply secure the old thread under the spokes, cut a new length, draw it up through the hole at the centre of the circle, and begin weaving where you left off.)

STEP 8: When you reach the edge of the disc, turn it to the back, pass the needle under the loop between each notch and lift it off the disc. Continue around the disc, lifting each loop off in turn, taking care not to let your yarn draw up too tightly.

STEP 9: Remove the button covering from the cardboard disc.

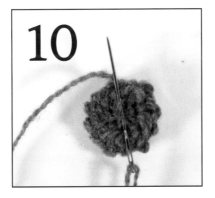

STEP 10: Place the button face down on the back of the button covering.

Carefully pull the yarn, drawing in the button-covering to conceal the back of the button. Make a few stitches across the back, securing, tightening and neatening the button covering so that the button is completely concealed.

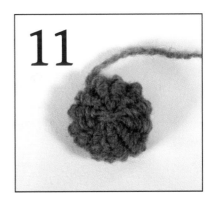

STEP 11: Retain a length of yarn for securing your button to the front of your tunic.

Button covers can be made in any size – just make sure to cut your cardboard disc about 2.5cm/1in larger than your buttons.

SPECIAL TECHNIQUES

THE RECOMMENDED YARN

The designs in this book were all created using one of my all-time favourite yarns – Jamieson & Smith's 2 ply Jumper Weight (which knits as a standard 4 ply). This yarn is produced from top-quality Shetland wool, hand-sorted and graded from the best local fleeces, with an impressive level of care shown at every processing stage. It is an ideal yarn for showcasing the simple stripes and colourwork patterns that feature in this book. The palette is rich and varied; the woollen-spun fibres hold together nicely; it blooms beautifully during blocking (lending your work the 'halo' characteristic of real Shetland wool); and the resulting fabric is durable and wears well.

If you use Jamieson & Smith's Jumper Weight for the projects in this book, you will create beautiful, professional-looking hand-knits that will last you for many years.

WATCH YOUR SWATCH!

Achieving the correct tension is essential. For your garment to have the best fit, you need to ensure that you are knitting at the correct number of stitches to the cm or inch.

Producing a swatch may be time-consuming, but it is a *crucial* stage of knitting many of the designs in this book. All of the garment patterns include detailed instructions on how to produce your swatches. These swatches will also allow you to familiarise yourself with the techniques involved in each pattern.

STEEKS
CUT YOUR STEEKS

'Steek' is simply a Shetland word for 'stitch'. In modern, commercial knitting patterns (namely, those that have been produced over the past thirty years or so) the word has shifted meaning, coming to to refer to the small bridge of 'waste' stitches that are often included in a design to allow the garment to be cut open after knitting (comparable to a seam allowance in sewing).

In the Ursula Cardigan and Scatness Tunic designs, the steek bridge enables you to knit the majority of the garment swiftly and seamlessly in the round. After knitting is complete, the bridges are reinforced, and simply cut down the centre, to create front and / or sleeve openings. Jamieson & Smith Jumper Weight is a 'sticky' yarn that most Shetland knitters would cut without fear of stitches unravelling. For peace of mind, however, I recommend reinforcing before cutting using the crocheted method (see below).

REINFORCING STEEKS WITH CROCHET

All steeks in this book are worked over 7 stitches. In the following instructions, these stitches are numbered 1 to 7 from right to left.

You will be working two columns of double crochet (US single crochet), the first between stitches 3 and 4, and the second between stitches 4 and 5. These two chains pull away from the centre (stitch 4), allowing you to cut easily and neatly.

1. Weave in all loose ends to the back of the work, away from stitch 4.
2. With strong sock yarn of similar shade to your garment, and a 2.5mm crochet hook, make a slip-knot and place it over your hook.
3. Push hook through bound-off edge of work through centre of stitch 3, draw a loop through fabric and slipknot to secure yarn (1 loop on hook).
4. Push hook through front leg of stitch 3 and back leg of stitch 4 (3 loops on hook).
5. Yarn over hook and pull through the knitted stitches (2 loops on hook)
6. Yarn over hook and pull through both loops on hook (1 loop on hook, and 1 reinforcement double crochet stitch made).
7. Continue in this way, repeating steps 4 to 6 for each row of the steek, pushing hook through front leg of stitch 3 and back leg of stitch 4 each time.
8. When you have worked your column of double crochet down each row, secure it to the cast-on edge of the steek through the centre of stitch 3, and fasten off.
9. Turn work 180 degrees.
10. Rejoin yarn to hook with slipknot; push hook through cast-on edge of work through centre of stitch 5, draw a loop through fabric and slipknot to secure yarn.
11. Push hook through front leg of stitch 4 and back leg of stitch 5 (3 loops on hook).
12. Yarn over hook and pull through the knitted stitches (2 loops on hook). Then yarn over hook and pull both

loops through (1 loop on hook and 1 reinforcement double crochet st made).

13 Continue working your second reinforcement in the same manner as the first, all the way up to the bound-off edge.

14 Press the two lines of double crochet gently away from each other, revealing a ladder of knitted strands running up the centre of stitch 4.

15 With a small, sharp pair of scissors, cut each strand of this ladder, taking care not to snip the crocheted reinforcement, or the other layer of knitted fabric.

Follow instructions in the pattern to stitch down and finish your steek edges after cutting.

For further information and illustrations, see the second of my steek tutorials online – follow the links from this page: **www.katedaviesdesigns. com/tutorials**

COLOURWORK TIPS

FAIR ISLE TECHNIQUE FOR COLOURWORK

Strand the yarn not in use loosely along the back of the work. If working two-handed, the 'foreground' yarn will usually be in your left hand, or be taken from below, if you are working one-handed. If your tension is even, there should be no need to 'catch' or 'weave' your stitches as is sometimes recommended.

COLOURWORK TENSION

To maintain an even tension when working colourwork over small circumferences (such as mittens), try turning the work inside out. The knit side will still be facing you (allowing you to work from the right side as usual), but the floats will be stretched around the work, easing up the tension.

CORRUGATED RIB

Also known as two-colour rib. Work as for Fair Isle colourwork, purling stitches where indicated and stranding the yarn not in use loosely along the back of the work.

BLOCKING AND FINISHING

For your hand-knits to look their best, they should be carefully wet-blocked, shaped and dried before wearing. Some of the designs included in this book involve finishing methods, such as sewing in a trim or zip, adding interior facings, or completing edges and cuffs with i-cord, all of which will lend your hand-knits a really professional look and are well-worth taking time over. Each pattern includes detailed instructions for relevant blocking and finishing methods.

SHORT ROWS

Two methods are described here. I recommend using the Carol Sunday Short Row technique (similar to Japanese short rows) when working the Ursula Cardigan sleeve caps. For raising the back of the neck on other patterns, I recommend the wrap and turn technique.

CAROL SUNDAY'S SHORT ROWS

To turn on both knit and purl sides

1 Work to the turning point.
2 Turn the work.
3 Return working yarn to the front (knit side) or back (purl side) as if to work next stitch.
4 Place one piece of contrasting yarn across the working yarn, marking the turning point.
5 Work the next stitch.

Continue to work along the row as usual. The contrasting yarn will remain as a placeholder.

To take in the next stitch and add another short row

On knit side:

1 Work up to the turning point (you will see a gap, and the contrasting thread of yarn running through the fabric underneath)
2 Insert left needle into the loop of yarn that has the contrasting thread running through it
3 Knit this loop together with the next stitch (k2tog).
4 Turn, following instructions above.

On purl side:

1 Work up to the turning point or gap.
2 Slip the next stitch purlwise onto your right needle.
3 Insert your left needle into the loop of yarn that has the contrasting thread running through it, lifting it up from the bottom.
4 Return slipped stitch to left needle.
5 Purl slipped stitch together with loop (p2tog).
6 Turn, following instructions above.

WRAP AND TURN SHORT ROWS
To turn on knit side

1 Knit to turning point.
2 Slip next stitch purlwise to right needle.
3 Bring the yarn to the front between the needles.
4 Return the slipped stitch to the left needle.
5 Bring the yarn to the back between the needles.
6 Turn work to purl side and continue.

To turn on purl side

1 Purl to turning point.
2 Slip next stitch purlwise to right needle.
3 Bring the yarn to the back of the work.
4 Return the slipped stitch to the left needle.
5 Bring the yarn to the front between the needles
6 Turn work to knit side and continue.

To close gap

1 Knit to the turning point. You will see a horizontal bar of yarn lying in front of the stitch that you slipped before you turned the work. This is the wrap.
2 Insert tip of right needle into both the wrap and the wrapped stitch and knit them together (this pushes the wrap to the back of the work and closes the gap).

CAST-ON AND BIND-OFF METHODS

I-CORD BIND-OFF (ALSO KNOWN AS APPLIED I-CORD)

Cast on 3 stitches using the cable cast-on method. *K2, k2tog tbl (the second of these stitches will be a garment stitch). Slip 3 stitches from right needle to left needle. Pull the working yarn across the back.* Repeat from * to *. At final 3 sts (when all garment stitches have been cast off), finish as follows: K1, k2tog tbl, slip 2 sts to left needle, k2tog, pull yarn through.

BACKWARDS-LOOP CAST-ON

Also known as the single cast on, loop cast on or E cast on. This simple cast-on method enables you to add-in sts without breaking the working yarn. *Loop working yarn over left thumb (making a shape like a lower case e), and place it on right needle backwards so that it does not unravel. Tighten.* Repeat from * to * for required number of sts.

PROVISIONAL CAST-ON

In these patterns, I describe a very simple method for casting on provisionally using a crochet chain. Casting on provisionally in this manner (preferably with a strong, smooth sock yarn) allows you unzip and pick up the 'live' stitches at a garment's edge in order to finish it neatly after knitting is complete. There are many alternative provisional cast-on methods. I particularly like this method described

by Lucy Neatby:
http://www.youtube.com/watch?v=R3J-sUx_whE
and Åsa's Winding Cast On (also known as a Turkish cast on):
http://asatricosa.wordpress.com/how-to/winding-provisional-cast-on/
You can find other good provisional cast-on methods described in Elizabeth Zimmermann's *Knitting Without Tears* (1995 edn) (invisible cast-on, page 20) and June Hemmons Hiatt's *Principles of Knitting* (2012 edn) (alternating provisional cast-on, pages 59-61). Feel free to use whichever provisional cast-on method you prefer.

SEWN BIND-OFF

A stretchy bind-off method should be used where a flexible edge is desirable, for example around ribbed cuffs, necklines, or shawl edges. Instructions are given here for the sewn bind-off, but feel free to use the decrease bind-off, or any other method you prefer.

1 Break yarn, leaving a tail at least 3 times as long as the bound-off edge. Thread the tail of the yarn onto a tapestry needle.
2 *Pass the tapestry needle purlwise through first two sts on left-hand needle. Pass needle knitwise through first st on left-hand needle, pull to an even tension and slip this stitch off the knitting needle.* Repeat from * to * until all sts have been bound off.

STITCHING

INVISIBLE SLIP STITCH OR BLIND STITCH

Slip stitches are used in the Scatness Tunic and Ursula Cardigan patterns to secure the button-band trim. You will need to use a very sharp sewing needle and fine, strong sewing thread. The bound edges of ribbon or lining trim are usually reinforced with a tiny hem or binding – you will use this binding to contain and disguise each stitch. After pinning out your trim as described in the pattern, secure your thread at one end. *Pass the needle through

the binding for 2mm, then, when it emerges, catch a a thread or two of the knitted fabric just *underneath* the trim.* Repeat from * to *.

BACK STITCH

Back stitch is a strong sewing stitch, used in the Scatness Tunic and Ursula Cardigan patterns to secure the cut edges of the steeks to the inside of front edges and armholes. Pin your steek edge into place, and secure your thread. Pull the needle through the steek edge, catch the knitted fabric, then double the needle back on itself. The needle should then emerge slightly beyond the stitch just made, before doubling back on itself again. When catching the knitted fabric, do so lightly, ensuring that your stitches do not show through to the front of the work.

PICKING UP STITCHES

PU: PICK UP WITHOUT KNITTING

Lift up live loop *without knitting* and place it on needle.

PUK: PICK UP AND KNIT

With working yarn, pick up the required number of new stitches *through* the knitted fabric (that is, push needle through to the *back* of the work, pick up a loop from the wrong side of the fabric, and draw through to the *right side* to create a new stitch).

PICKING UP STITCHES BESIDE A STEEK BRIDGE

When picking up stitches for a button band or sleeves, where a steek bridge has been worked, you should ensure that none of the bridge shows through on the right side. To do this, simply pick up your stitches in the space *between* the final main pattern stitch and the first stitch of the bridge. Your picked up stitches will lie flush against the main pattern, and those of your bridge will be hidden away at the back of the work (to see this in action, take a look at the third of my steek tutorials, following the links from this page:
www.katedaviesdesigns.com/tutorials

GRAFTING

KITCHENER STITCH

These instructions are for grafting in stocking stitch.

First, thread a tapestry needle with 60cm/24in length of working yarn.

1 Hold knitting needle tips parallel to one another, with right sides of work outermost.
2 Insert tapestry needle **purlwise** into first stitch on front needle. Pull yarn through.
3 Insert tapestry needle **knitwise** into the first stitch on back needle. Pull yarn through.
4 Insert tapestry needle **knitwise** into first stitch on front needle, slipping stitch off needle.
5 Insert tapestry needle **purlwise** into next stitch on front needle. Pull yarn through.
6 Insert tapestry needle **purlwise** into first stitch on back needle, slipping stitch off needle.
7 Insert tapestry needle **knitwise** into next stitch on back needle. Pull yarn through.
8 Repeat steps 4-7 until all stitches have been grafted together.

FOR GENERAL REFERENCE

June Hemmons Hiatt
The Principles of Knitting (2012 edn)
Margaret Radcliffe
The Knitting Answer Book (2006)
Montse Stanley
The Handknitter's Handbook (2001 edn)
Elizabeth Zimmermann
Knitting Without Tears (1995 edn)

GLOSSARY

Bind off	UK cast off
Stocking stitch	US stockinette stitch
Tension	US gauge
Facing	A layer of fabric used to reinforce and strengthen the interior of a hem or edging
Sock yarn	A smooth yarn of 4 ply weight (US fingering weight), usually made from a blend of wool and nylon
Tapestry needle	A sewing needle suitable for wool, with a blunt tip

ABBREVIATIONS

CC1(2,3)	contrast colour 1 (2, 3)
cm	centimetres
cont	continued
dpn(s)	double-pointed needle(s)
foll	follows/following
g	grams
in	inches
K	knit
k2tog	knit next 2 stitches together (1 stitch decreased)
k3tog	knit next 3 stitches together (2 stitches decreased)
kfb	knit into the front and back of the same stitch (1 stitch increased)
lh	left-hand
m	metres
m1	lift bar between sts from front to back and knit through the back of this loop (1 stitch increased)
MC	main colour
mm	millimetres
P	purl
p2sso	pass two slipped stitches over
pm(A, B, etc)	place marker(A, B, etc)
pu	pick up (see **Special Techniques**)
puk	pick up and knit (see **Special Techniques**)
rh	right-hand
RS	right side
sl	slip a stitch purlwise unless otherwise noted
slm(A, B, etc)	slip marker(A, B, etc)
ssk	slip 2 stitches knitwise one at a time, knit 2 slipped stitches together through back of loop (1 stitch decreased)
sssk	slip 3 stitches knitwise one at a time, knit 3 stitches together through back of loop (2 stitches decreased)
st(s)	stitch(es)
tbl	through the back loops
WS	wrong side
yds	yards
yo	yarn over

ACKNOWLEDGMENTS

TOM BARR

Tom is my amazing, multi-talented partner, who shares everything with me, including a dry northern sensibility, a deep love of Britain's wild places and a fondness for pootling around in a camper van. He is also a superb photographer and is particularly good at taking pictures of knitwear. Tom is responsible for the garment photography in this book.

BRUCE

One of the great pleasures of working independently is spending my days with Bruce, my fun-loving and indispensable labrador companion. Bruce also enjoys Shetland and has shared many fine walks there with Tom and I.

MELANIE IRELAND

This book would really not have been possible without Mel. An incredible knitter and a wonderful friend, she test-knits most of my designs and is also responsible for bringing me back down to earth when my ideas turn batty and unrealistic.

JEN ARNALL-CULLIFORD

I have learnt masses about being a design professional from Jen. She is this book's technical editor and general sage. I can think of no one with whom I'd rather share my virtual office: she is the sharpest and funniest knitting geek I know.
www.jenacknitwear.co.uk

NIC BLACKMORE

Nic is responsible for this book looking completely beautiful, and for giving me a little thrill every time I turn its pages. Nic has not only shared my creative vision for this book, but with her own vital spark, has made it come to life. I suspect she doesn't know just how talented she is.
www.laliloo.squarespace.com

SARAH LAURENSON

I met Sarah on my first visit to Shetland, when she was at Jamieson & Smith. There is no-one working in this industry quite like Sarah: she has a knack of just making amazing things happen without making any sort of fuss about it. She also designs and makes breathtakingly beautiful things, as you can see at **www.reformlane.co.uk**

AND A BIG SHOUT-OUT TO...

My friends at Jamieson & Smith and Curtis Wool, for supporting this project with 100% Real Shetland wool: Martin Curtis, Ella Gordon, Oliver Henry, Sandra Manson, and June Moulder. **www.shetlandwoolbrokers.co.uk**
My friends at Promote Shetland, who have encouraged me and permitted me to reproduce many beautiful photographs from their archives: Misa Hay and Deborah Legatte. **www.shetland.org**
Chris Dyer and Jane Outram, whose knowledge and enthusiasm inspired the Scatness designs, and Anna NicGuaire for her help with Gaelic puffin names.
John Moncrieff, for inspirational wildlife photography **www.johnmoncrieffphotography.zenfolio.com**
And finally, everyone at Shetland Museum and Archives and Shetland Amenity Trust, whose work to preserve and interpret the history and heritage of Shetland is both heartening and exemplary.
www.shetlandamenity.org
www.shetland-museum.org.uk

THE TEAM

Publisher & Author:	Kate Davies
Technical Editor:	Jen Arnall-Culliford
Art & Production Editor:	Nic Blackmore
Photography:	Tom Barr
Test Knitting:	Melanie Ireland
Yarn Support:	Jamieson & Smith

COLOURS OF SHETLAND

First published in 2012 by Kate Davies Designs Ltd, Box 161, MBE, 12 South Bridge, Edinburgh EH1 1DD
© Copyright Kate Davies Designs Ltd 2012

Printed by Williams Press, Berkshire, UK

British Library Cataloguing in Publication Data:
A catalogue record for this book is available from the British Library. ISBN-978-0-9574666-0-9